Lauren &

Have a wonderful
together —
Brad 2018

MW01595681

Goodnight Gorgeous

When the
heart
you love   is the one
you just
broke...

BRAD C. ENGEL

Books Recommended by Brad

(Books by DUKE CHARLES)

LUKE KASH WESTERN SERIES

People of the Horse
Spirit and the Blood
Blood and Thunder
Thunder Cloud and Spirit Walker

ROC REESE MYSTERY SERIES

Birdies and San Diego Heat
Birdies and Vegas Heat
Birdies and Gulf Coast Heat
Birdies and New Orleans Heat

ELI GIDEON SERIES

Gideon, Bounty Hunter

...and anything written by Brad C. Engel

OTHER BOOKS BY BRAD C. ENGEL

BRAD C. ENGEL

Bethel1808 Publishers
Lewisville, Texas

For information about this title or to order other books and/or electronic media, contact the publisher:

Bethel1808
Lewisville, TX 75057
www.BradCEngel.com
bethel1808@gmail.com
ISBNs for Goodnight Gorgeous

Softcover: 978-1-947201-90-3
eBook: 978-1-947201-00-2

Printed in the United States of America
Cover and Interior design: Bethel1808

Dedication

To Laura,
the love of my life;
you are,
always have been and
always will be...

Gorgeous

Acknowledgements

I would like to extend many many thanks to my editor: you always make me look and sound so good. I truly appreciate all the work you put into this project and having dinner with you every night was so wonderful.

Thanks to my best friend and encourager: you pushed me softly but held me to my goals. As I would read to you looking for praise, you always had the perfect answer, "I love it, but we'll change it all!" Thank you so much for keeping me on track and on time. You are truly the most remarkable woman I have ever met.

And a special thanks to my co-author in this book and in life: you helped me with the big words and kept me from writing things that people might take wrong like, "...you're an idiot!" I didn't understand it when you told me that people might get offended, but I guess now I see (Not really, but you are usually right about these things). You truly are the best co-author I could have, and you are so smokin' hot! (I want credit for saying this.)

You three ladies are the only woman I have ever loved.

Very truly,
Brad

Table of Contents

Author's Note

Contemplating the writing of this book I met with family, friends and colleagues who all thought it would be a great idea, or at least that is what they told me, so I ventured out. As I approached the end of the writing and editing portion of <u>Knock It Off and Go To Sleep</u>, the original title of this book, I met with my publisher to gain direction on moving forward. After reviewing his copy, he told me to change the title and then he imparted wisdom to me that I will always cherish:

"Wow! This may be the worst book I have ever read. Nobody is going to buy anything else you write...ever."

What great advice. I could tell he really spent some time coming up with such deep insight. I took it to heart and realized that I had better include everything I want to say in this book, since I may never write another one; so I included

Brad's Shorts

Every couple of chapters, I inserted short stories of my life with Laura. They are just for fun and really don't have anything to do with the point of this book; but my publisher couldn't stop me from adding them, although he tried really hard.

I hope they minister to you.

Introduction

I love to work in my yard. Almost every time I do, I feel like the Lord speaks to me. It never ceases to amaze me how God brings such deep spiritual revelations through our observing natural things. I see His beauty and power in creation, and I marvel at how wise He is. I feel so loved and important when I take a closer look at things that I used to busily rush past, and see how intricate and how captivating He designed nature, just for me to marvel at and enjoy.

I love how it feels to be impressed!
I love how it feels to be loved!

Have you ever walked by one of those gardens that just makes you stop and stare; one of those gardens that makes you wish you could grow such luscious tomatoes, such abundant lettuces, such amazing flowers and trees? The vibrant hues, the alluring fragrances, the indescribable shapes and textures--your senses can't even take in all its beauty! Well, I'd love to be an expert gardener, but I'm not. One thing I *do* know from my limited gardening experiences: the soil makes all the difference.

As I sit here trying to think of all the "soil" terms I know to really bring this home, all I can think of are: nitrogen content, peat moss, potting soil, clay…oh well. I'm so happy that God gives His deep wisdom even to the unlearned. What I *do* know is that good fruit grows from good soil, and for years and years, the soil of my heart had been the *bad* soil of fear. I don't think it takes long to envision the kind of fruit that grows *very* well in this soil: insecurity, judgment, performance, condemnation, anger, dread, depression, guilt, rejection, resentment, criticism, inadequacy, meanness and fear itself. I think you understand. I hate the thought of anyone in my life having to take and eat of any of these fruits. Sadly, my husband was among those, and our marriage was a dark place for many years. We were miserable; and as hard as we seemed to try, we just grew more miserable.

As a Christian, I tried so hard to change my fruit, misunderstanding scriptures like, "…every good tree bears good fruit, but a bad tree bears bad fruit. A good tree cannot bear bad fruit, nor can a bad tree bear good fruit. Every tree that does not bear good fruit is cut down and thrown into the fire. Therefore, by their fruits you will know them," (Matt. 7:17-20).

Yikes! As I looked at my life, at my fruit, I knew I was surely one of the ones who would be cut down and….

The harder I tried, the worse I felt. Deep, profound panic and condemnation grew even taller in me.

I find myself in tears sitting here remembering the prison where I used to live; and where I would still be,

But God....

Now, I can't worship hard enough; I can't proclaim loudly or often enough; I can't praise or thank Him enough!

Now, it's so easy for me to see Him as a loving Father Who loves to be with me; Who loves to daily lavish me with unending benefits.

Now, it's so easy for me to see Him as an adoring Husband Who longs for me; Who is captivated by me; Who loves to show off to impress me and to rescue me: my Knight in shining armor!

Now, it's so easy for me to see Him as my Best Friend, Whom I can fully be myself around; Who loves to make me laugh; Who lives to help me and to crush all my fears.

You know, what I didn't really expect...was that God would reveal Himself to me as so many of these things THROUGH my husband. This beautiful book details the story of our life together, and of the things God taught him about how to love a bride.

As I sat the other day, all these years later, once again pondering the idea of our fruit, I couldn't help but marvel at the abundance of good fruit that has so naturally emerged in us. I was amazed at the profound joy that is ours, the peace that passes understanding and our security in the love of God. I was overwhelmed by our confidence in our identity and position in Christ, the love and compassion we have for each other and others, and the passion in us to see others knowing the freedom and abundant life of Christ. This good fruit that only the Spirit of God can produce has been so abundant that others have been able to be blessed by it too! That day I heard God say, "I've changed the soil of your heart." In an instant, I realized that He had been replacing my soil of fear with the soil of love all these years through the love of my husband for me. God has been loving me through my husband, and the soil of love has made ALL the difference in my life!

Our marriages are a picture of the relationship between Jesus and His Church, His bride. However, I didn't even have a clue what He would teach and impart to us about this profound truth. He intends to heal us through our marriages, to reveal Himself through our marriages, and to display to the world His nature and His glory through our marriages.

I am constantly astounded by this ever-deepening revelation! Every day it just keeps getting better and better, and it can for you too. We pray that as you read this book, the Spirit of wisdom and revelation in the knowledge of Him be given to you and your precious spouse.

Look to Him. Trust Him. He is "...able to do exceedingly abundantly above all that we ask or think according to the power that works in us." (Eph 3:20)

Laura Engel,
Proud, blessed wife of Brad C. Engel

Chapter One
"Yeah, but Your Wife's a Hottie!"

A few years back, I was a member of a men's trip. You know the kind I'm talking about: guys get out with other guys, away from work, away from family and just relax and kick back out in the woods around a campfire, breaking branches off trees, hiking trails and all kinds of "man things." This trip had a special purpose, though. It was a trip put on by the Men's Ministry of our church and we were supposed to get in touch with our emotions and our feelings. There were planned times to sit and talk; to reach out and be vulnerable and let other guys see your weaknesses. We were supposed to "try and dig deep and really express to the other guys how you feel about things." I was supposed to show the chinks in my armor, to expose my jugular and be confident in the fact that I am in a "safe place."

I hate this kind of stuff. The only time I have feelings around other men is when I am leaping into the air off the perfectly manicured Bermuda grass on the 18th green, and I just rolled a 20-foot putt that hit the bottom of the cup so soundly that the rumble in the earth was felt all the way back in the clubhouse. Other than that, I don't have feelings. I know this because my wife spent the better part of the first years of our marriage asking me about them. I was young and very eager to impress her so I struggled with all that is in me to come up with my real feelings. Finally, reaching a point of clarity, I was able to adequately express how I truly felt.

"I feel fine!"

That's pretty much the mantra of the American male in today's society. We think it. We live it. We breathe it. If we got together for afternoon tea and crumpets, we would discuss it; and if we held weekly American Male Meetings, we would recite it right after the Pledge of Allegiance. Hear my roar, "I am an American male and I feel fine!"

On the second night of this particular men's trip, sitting around the campfire in some unstructured time, the discussion began to center around our wives. It's not really surprising that this subject would come up. It is the single most important physical thing in a man's life, whether he will admit it or not.

This wasn't really an emotional discussion, but rather an opportunity to whine and gripe about the women in our lives, and in some cases, the women no longer in our lives. It usually only takes one person's negative opinion to get a conversation going in a negative way. Because we are men and don't really get in touch with our feelings, it is really easy to just agree or add to the current conversation. We may think of a few good things to say just to be a part of the conversation and not even realize that we don't really agree with what we are actually saying.

The discussion went in a pretty disheartening direction, and as I listened to these guys describe the problems they have with their wives, I began thinking about my wife. I realized that I am really lucky. Actually, it's more than that. I am truly blessed. As I was hearing stories about how this guy's wife is always fighting with him to clean up after himself, and how that guy's wife is so bossy, I realized that Laura is such a great wife. One guy said his wife doesn't respect him, and told him as much. Another guy said his wife was no longer attracted to him. Most of the other guys mumbled in agreement, some even commenting about the lack of sex in their marriages. I remembered being just like them.

Fifteen years earlier, I would have had plenty to say about my wife. She would argue and disagree with me too often. After all, "I am the man here and what I say goes." She wasn't nearly as attracted to me as I thought she should be. She wore her old "comfortable" clothes when she was with me, and then would get dressed up do her hair and makeup to go see friends. I felt tricked. Marriage was supposed to be the next step after dating. The next step is supposed to be better, not worse. That is why it is the next step. If things were supposed to get worse, nobody in their right mind would ever take the next step.

Laura even told me one time that if she had to do it all over again, she wouldn't marry me...but that was years ago.

Sitting there quietly eventually got me noticed. In this group of friends, I was the only one not saying anything. One guy sitting directly across from me caught my eye. He didn't say anything, but he was watching with a deep, inquisitive stare. I could tell that he was trying to figure me out. He knew I didn't agree. They could all see it on my face, but what should he do about it? Should he stop talking and join me in quiet support of our wives, or should he confront me for not being a part of the group? Seeing the struggle in his mind, I decided to let him off the hook.

"You know guys; it occurs to me that you all liked your wives when you were dating. Maybe if you still liked them, they would still like you."

Total silence.... Every guy looked right at me. Time moved very slowly. We were supposed to have each others' backs. We don't question each other and we sure don't accuse any man, especially a friend, of being at fault in his marriage. Who did I think I was?

Then something happened. The guy sitting there across the campfire from me bowed up, sat up straight and said, "That's easy for you to say. You're married to a hottie!" Almost in perfect unison, the other men jumped in and agreed. This was the second time that a group of guys told me that my wife was a hottie.

The first time was earlier that same year when I was leading a group of college-age guys on a mission trip, and had opened up a discussion about business and life. Trying to sound really wise, I offered to give them a little advice that I wish someone had given me. I talked about the value of hard work, explaining that Proverbs 14:23 says, "All hard work brings a profit..."(New International Version). I just knew I was going to leave a legacy in these college guys. I was imparting my wisdom to them about the important things of life, when one of them said they had been talking and wanted to ask me a question. They all wanted to know what the trick was to marrying such a hottie. I thought they were trying to rattle me so I played along, until I realized that they were actually serious. They thought my wife was not just pretty, but an actual HOTTIE.

This was incredible. First, all those college guys said it, and now these guys around the campfire. I knew that I thought my wife was hot, but to hear it from others was such a great boost to my ego. I knew I had married up. I knew how really gorgeous my wife was, but I hadn't realized everybody else saw it too. It wasn't just blind love in me. She was now a trophy wife! I had arm candy! She was smart. She was beautiful. She walked with confidence. She was officially a hottie!

With the dark sky above and the night lit only by the glow of the campfire, I sat up and continued trying to steer the conversation in a new direction; knowing I had already set myself at odds with most, if not all, of these guys. I answered with boldness in my voice and a confidence inside me that was planted, fertilized and watered by my extremely hot wife who thinks I have the answers to most of the world's problems.

"My wife is a hottie because I made her a hottie. The question you should be asking is, why isn't yours?" This drew out a few mumbles and snarls but mostly hushed puzzled looks.

I continued, "When a professional football team doesn't win for an extended period, do they fire all the players or do they fire the coach? When a company's stock is not performing well, does the board fire all the employees or the CEO?"

I stated plainly that, "God only makes one kind of woman: hotties! He made your wife exactly the way He wanted her. This world, harsh words, bad days, all kinds of negative influences and so many other things have corrupted her looks, feelings, attitude, confidence and everything else it could get to...and we are supposed to be their safe place, their protector, their encouragement. It's not just our job; it's our destiny to help them become what God has created them to be. God has put these women in our care, and one of these days we will stand before Him and give an account of what we did with the gifts that He gave us. You see, you guys don't know the whole story."

I went on to explain how my wife became the hottie that they see, and how much work it took, and still takes, every day...and it all started when God said to tell her,

"Goodnight Gorgeous."

Chapter Two
The Bus Stops Here

I was standing at the corner waiting for the school bus as I had many times before. I was a junior at Coronado High School in El Paso, Texas. I could not wait to get my own car. I hated the bus; not just because of the hour that the bus took to get to my destination just 3.3 miles away, but also because of the reputation I was acquiring, or lack thereof. My own car would give me freedom, status and presence. I knew that when I drove up in my own car, to my private parking spot that the school was sure to give me, it would be eye-catching and jaw-dropping. The world would stop and take notice when I had my own car. For now, my parents would let me drive the family car on rare occasions. It was a big orange Ford E150 van with oversized tires. Sometimes, I got to drive the other van: a plumbing service vehicle from my dad's company. I didn't mind, at least I had wheels...just not today. No, today I was sentenced to ride with the other wheel-less kids that couldn't afford their own car.

That's when I saw her.

Across the street a car pulled up near the bus stop; not too close—about two houses down—obviously transporting another person that had to ride the bus but didn't want to be dropped off until the last possible second. I looked up Frontera Road and saw the big yellow beast coming to pick us up. She must have seen it too, because that is when the back door of the four-wheel-drive AMC Eagle station-wagon opened.

As I watched, I saw under the door a very sexy leg with a short ankle-high white sock and white tennis shoe touch the ground. As she continued out of the car, almost in slow motion, I noticed her green long-sleeved sweatshirt. That made sense with the cool weather we were having. I had gotten there early and had been standing at the bus stop for about twenty minutes. Of course, I had noticed the cold. I had to walk about ten miles uphill in the snow, across traffic and through the briar patch to get there and my timing was sometimes off. Okay, maybe it wasn't that bad, but I had to walk. I could be early, but never late. My dad would hit the roof if I missed the bus...it only happened one time.

Then I saw the most amazing thing. This gorgeous girl getting out of the car across the street appeared in full and was wearing...a miniskirt.

"I'm going to marry those legs!" I said, and then realized that I was speaking out loud. All the other kids at the bus stop looked at me. I didn't care...she was as good as mine. Yes, she was a stranger; yes, I was a dork on a bus; and yes, I had a girlfriend. All of that was meaningless. She was gorgeous and I was going to spend the rest of my life telling her so.

As she approached the bus, I decided to let her get on first so I could follow her to her seat and hopefully sit with her.

She found her seat and I sat in the seat right in front of her. Of course, I turned around to talk. I teased her about everything from her miniskirt to being driven to the bus stop when she lived only eight houses away. She was a princess, and although most of my teasing was about this, I loved that about her. Her personality matched her beauty and I was captured. We began hanging out at lunch, after school, before school, at the football games; you name it, we were together. She had my attention. Soon we became best friends and, although I never really liked being in the "Friend-Zone," I was fine with this...as long as I could be near her.

I quickly terminated the relationship I had with my current girlfriend. She was a college girl at UTEP who began enjoying her new-found college freedom from her parents...and from me. Perfect timing!

But unfortunately, the love of my life, the future mother of my children, the most beautiful woman in the world, began dating my good friend, Mike.

I hated Mike.

Actually, I didn't hate him. He was a good friend, but for all practical purposes I had to hate him; he was dating my wife...well future wife. This actually worked out well for me since Mike was from a very religious family. He really didn't believe in being very aggressive in his relationships; he rarely even held Laura's hand. They were really great together but obviously he would have to die, or at least break up with her. Of course, I couldn't be the one to break them up. That would be wrong. But, surely the God of Abraham, Isaac and Jacob could understand my problem and send His mighty wrath down to smite Mike...or break them up...whatever God wanted to do to him was fine. Long story short, I prayed, it worked. She broke up with him. Hallelujah! I had to move fast. She was available and I was not going to let this chance go by. I raced in and ran to her side to comfort her in the midst of such a devastating heartbreak.

I offered, "Oh, you poor thing...I'm here...there, there," and whatever else I could think of to ease her pain. Finally, I had put in the time, addressed all the issues, calmed all the fears, dried all the tears and was ready to discuss the giant elephant in the room...she should be mine!

I found the perfect time and place and asked her to be my girlfriend. I knew she liked me and I knew that she knew that I liked her. It would be perfect. We were made for each other.

It took almost no time for her to answer. You could tell she had been thinking about it for as long as I had. I barely got the question out when she said,
"NO."

She had some really great reason that I don't remember because it was a stupid answer. The correct answer was "yes" and it would take the next six months and all of my attention to get to that answer. My grades at school dropped from their normal

position of Cs and Ds to "I don't even care." There was only one thing that I wanted; and I eventually got it. She said, "Yes" and we lived happily ever after....
Actually, I'm getting a little ahead of myself.

Everything was good for a while. We fell in love and we were happy. She learned that she could trust me and began to, more and more. We went to church all the time and got very involved in the youth group. Most of our dates were part of church activities. We were the good kids. In fact, our youth group began a new program for student leaders. Everyone voted and I was chosen as President of the youth group and Laura as Secretary. Even some of our teachers at school, who also attended our church, began to know us as good kids. Everything looked great, seemed great and felt great; but there were deeper issues that hadn't begun to surface yet.

I had always wanted to be a pastor. I had seen a lot of them and it looked like a great job. I knew that I loved God and I felt like this was my "calling."

Laura knew exactly where she was headed: college and medical school. Her father was a doctor, her mother was a nurse, her grandfather was a doctor, her grandmother was a pharmacist, her uncles were doctors, her step-mother was a nurse and her step-father was a veterinarian. She had a little bit of pressure and always knew where she was being pushed. All of this pressure may have even been self-inflicted, but it was still very real to her. There was a standard, and Laura never felt like she measured up.

This great love/friendship went on for about a year and I grew more and more ready to take our relationship to the next level: not marriage, sex.

I began pressuring her and she eventually gave in to me. We loved each other and became each other's safe place. Don't get me wrong, I wasn't a bad guy. I just knew I wanted to spend the rest of my life with her and she knew I would never hurt her. So, I rationalized that it was okay for us to "make love." I would always refer to it as "making love." It just sounded better; more justification on my part.

Not long after that, we found out that Laura was pregnant. So many feelings, so much fear, but I knew I could handle this. Yes, we were two teenagers about to be parents with no income and no idea how we were going to make it; but this is when I realized that I actually did love Laura. I wanted to be with her more than anything. I wanted this child. I had no idea what to do, but I knew I could do it; and I knew she trusted me, so we were going to be just fine...after all, we loved each other.

But the situation was so much worse than I realized.

Brad's Shorts

Coincidentally...About Brad's Shorts

A *good friend of mine used to be a Special Investigator for a department of the government that I am not sure I am allowed to mention, but it's known by three letters. He used to tell me tricks and techniques for getting to know people without them realizing that they are a target. I love this kind of stuff. I have always pictured myself as a covert operative much in the likes of Jason Bourne or James Bond.*

"Engel...Brad Engel."

He had ways to get people to open up and talk, and ways to just make people feel more comfortable.

One of these strategies was to discuss an issue just slightly out of their comfort zone. It made them look at you as "not so perfect" and allowed them to see you just as normal as they see themselves. This seemed right up my alley, so I decided to implement this technique one night in a small group meeting that was at our house.

These were all good Christian people that I wanted to impress. Some were businessmen and women, and some were in the ministry. Most were friends or at least acquaintances. We served coffee and snacks as we just visited.

As we gathered together in a group in the living room, a somewhat shy and classy lady whispered to me a question that makes people feel uncomfortable....

"May I use your restroom?"

"Of course," I said out loud. "It's just down the hall, second door on the right."

I should have stopped right there, but I realized this is that perfect opportunity to make an impact.

"Don't pay any attention to the underwear on the floor in there," as if my wife had not cleaned today. I knew my wife kept a perfect house. She would never let dirty clothes be seen laying anywhere, especially with company coming over.

I'm not sure why I said that, but it seemed to get the desired reaction. The lady asking the question smiled, knowing that nobody would ever leave underwear in the bathroom before a party. Other people in the group laughed and my wife had the perfect blend of a smirk and a smile while she rolled her eyes. It was conversational perfection. I could not have planned it better.

Throughout the evening, other people used the restroom, and each time someone did, laughter ensued; at first from my comments, but soon everyone was joining in on the jokes. The night was a great success. I was already looking forward to our next evening social. I sat in my chair thinking about how organizations are probably going to want to hire me to teach them how to have a great social gathering. Books will most likely be written about me and the techniques I employ. I became curious; could this incredible social skill be taught or is it something that just comes so naturally to me? I wondered whom Hollywood would get to play me in the movie that they will most likely make about my life.

I locked up for the evening and went in to kiss the kids goodnight. As I was coming out of my daughter's room, I turned to go into the hallway bathroom and make sure everything was still in order. I approached the door and the shelf in the hallway caught my eye. It was an 80's country-style shelf mounted just below eye level, about 18 inches long with three shaped pegs under it to hang things on. My wife usually had a cute tiny framed verse from the Bible hanging here, or some sort of dried flowers bundled and hung upside down.

Today, there were no dead flowers. Today, there was no cute Bible verse. No, today, there was just one thing hanging from the middle peg: my underwear.

Laura began teaching me early in our marriage that my clothes needed to make it into the clothes hamper. She would hang my underwear in the hallway as a joke and let me find them, just to emphasize the importance of the hamper in her laundry process. She would always threaten to leave them out for guests to see. I wasn't an idiot. I knew Laura would never, ever, ever allow anyone to think that she does not keep a perfectly clean house. I was safe. But...something had gone horribly wrong.

"LAURA!" I yelled and she came running.

"Did you put these here?" I asked.

I could see on her face that her mind was racing to figure out when my underwear were placed strategically under the shelf in the hallway.

"Have they been here all night?" I asked as she began to crack a smile.

She broke into laughter and confirmed that she had placed them there this morning.

"How could you...?"

Recalling the evening's events, she began laughing hysterically. As she walked away, she stood up a little straighter and even had a bit of confidence in her stride. I stood there stunned as I heard her say,

"...and that's how we learn."

Chapter Three
Broken Hearts Can't Be Wild

I was eighteen years old and about to be a father. I didn't grow up in one of those ooey-gooey, "Leave it to Beaver" kind of homes where everybody just knew that they were loved; but I never doubted my heavenly Father's love. I knew He loved me and would always take care of me. I had read all of the Bible verses that said He loves me and knew all the Bible stories of His incredible blessings for those that accept Him. But it was more than that. Just a few years earlier I had an encounter with the One True God.

I was lying in my bed one night listening to a praise and worship song as I did every night to fall asleep. As the music broke through, I really began thinking about the words.

"...was when He ran to me, He took me in His arms, held my head to His chest, said

'My son's come home again!' lifted my face,
wiped the tears from my eyes, with
forgiveness in His voice He said, 'Son, do you
know I still love you?'"

From that day on, I have always known that God loves me and would always forgive me. All the Bible verses I had ever learned began to make sense. I now saw everything through a lens of Him loving me. God began teaching me how to trust Him, and even more important, how to believe Him. This is when I learned the first deep principle that God showed me....

"You are my favorite child."

I knew it. Yes, He loves all of us, but I was His favorite. I remembered the parable of the lost sheep.

**"If a man has a hundred sheep, and
one of them goes astray, does he not
leave the ninety-nine and go to the
mountains to seek the one that is
straying? And if he should find it,
assuredly, I say to you, he rejoices more
over that sheep, than over the ninety-
nine that did not go astray."
(Matthew 18:12-13)**

It didn't say that He went and found another shepherd to watch the other sheep. It didn't say that He made sure there was no dangerous animal around that would attack the other sheep. It said that He left the others to go find the one lost sheep...that was me! You would only do this for your favorite one; and I was His favorite. I was so loved, and I never, ever forgot it.

I knew that the situation I was in was too big for me but I also knew that with God, all things are possible, and that took so much of the pressure off. I knew that Laura and I would be just fine. In fact, we would be better than fine; we would be great. I didn't realize that everybody didn't see it this way.

Laura was devastated. She had to face her family: aunts, uncles, grandparents, mom, and most terrifying...dad. This "A student" thought at the time that she had received the final grade on her life..."F."

So she, and sometimes we, faced the music. I wouldn't realize until later how torturous this was for her, but I knew that I could take care of her. I knew that she and I had a future together, and I knew that she trusted me; so I figured we would just get past this little issue and move on to preparing for a baby, a family, a life. That's when I began to realize that I no longer had her trust. I was confused, truly.

I thought to myself, "So, you made a mistake. So you think that your family won't forgive you...big deal. You can get over it. Actually, they can get over it 'cause we are going to be happy. We love each other and that is all we really need."

We talked a lot in the next few months. We had so much input from family and friends, and so much disappointment was heard in their voices. We moved very slowly. I asked her to marry me and we moved forward...actually I never asked, I just assumed. The wedding was planned and executed in a somewhat quiet and conservative form. It was the strategic solution to a problem. People showed up and observed the ceremony, but it wasn't really a celebration. I wasn't the obvious choice for a fit into Laura's broken family, especially now with the situation I had caused. It was never actually said, but I knew it and Laura definitely knew it. She wanted to love me but the problems I was causing just kept mounting up, to the point that Laura didn't even know exactly why, but she knew that she couldn't love, respect or trust me.

Laura's parent's got divorced when she was about seven years old. Her dad was in his residency in medical school and her mom worked as a nurse. Laura and her mom ended up moving to El Paso, while her dad lived in Dallas. He eventually got remarried and began his new family. About this same time, Laura's mom got remarried too and they began their new family. Babies started appearing in each family and Laura was going to be the big sister, but it wasn't long before she felt like she wasn't really a part of either family. She didn't really fit. She was the previous child, from a previous marriage. Those words cut deep. Nobody meant them as hurtful, but to Laura they were. Overwhelmed by insecurity, she became obsessed with making sure that her mom and dad were pleased with her, no matter what. She would continue this inner-battle for years to come.

Then some good-looking guy in high school invited her to church. Soon after that she met Jesus Christ, Who loved her no matter what... as long as she was good...or so she believed. Laura liked the idea that God loved her, and to a point, replaced her dad with

God. It was kind of like a "Do-Over." She could try again, and this time she would try harder to get it right.

It worked for a while because, although she felt like God was unhappy at her, he wasn't physically standing there in front of her, facing her with a disappointed look on His face. Plus, there was the advantage of thinking that God would forgive her. She knew that the Bible said He would, and sometimes she got really close to believing it...but only close to believing. In her mind, Laura had just added one more person in her life that she could disappoint.

After the wedding, we moved away to Plainview, Texas. I got a job as a Counselor-in-Training with MHMR of Texas and worked every afternoon and evening. I had my mornings free, so I enrolled at Wayland Baptist University. We found a little house just off campus and Laura stayed home to watch our beautiful daughter. Things were looking great. We were broke financially, but we had a lot of hand-me-down furniture and a car that ran...a great start.

Everything looked fine for a while. Our families knew that this was a train wreck in progress but politely held their tongues, or maybe they just didn't know how to help us. But to the local outside world, we looked great. We began going to a church, and even visited a few Bible study home groups. I had this marriage thing figured out. The first year was hard, but everything is hard at first. I knew that as we got our footing, things would get better. I kept trying to make our life exciting, fun, even wild. I thought that if I could make Laura happy, everything would be just fine. I would plan events and outings on the weekends, but we were in Plainview, Texas, and they still rolled up the streets at five o'clock. So we would go to Lubbock or Amarillo for the day. I just knew that eventually our life was going to be fun and exciting, and I would feel the love that I knew was in there somewhere. I knew that she would grow to love me more, but in reality, I didn't even know what the problem was. Then I began to get a clue.

We would argue and fight. We never got mean and we never got physical, but it was definitely hurtful. I would say things that I didn't mean and cut really deep into this woman that I claimed to love. I had a very sarcastic battle stick and I would use it to win every fight. If she was ever out-fighting me, I would just get louder and more dominating. I was harsh.

I could get over those feelings pretty quickly and calm down fairly easily; she couldn't. That's when the real hurtful words began. I would make jokes that were cutting. I didn't mean it; I was just trying to get a laugh. I was really good at joking. My jokes weren't very good, but I thought I was good at them. Laura would often tell me how hurtful the jokes I made were, but I couldn't take her word for it; she's biased. I told her to lighten up and that she just needs to get a better sense of humor. I told her that this is how God made me and He knew what He was doing. That's when God broke in again and told me about the power of my tongue.

"Why are you doing that?"

"Doing what?"

*"Why are you treating
my princess that way?"*

"Did you see what she did?"

"I'm talking to you."

"I don't know," I said hanging my head in shame.

"I don't know" was always my go-to answer. I
remember the conversations with my dad so many
times growing up. He was a big man that stood about
nine and a half feet tall, and he was always carrying a
paddle; at least that is how I saw him back then. I knew
there was no winning a discussion with him and I
knew I couldn't win this one either.

*"Your words have
the power of life and
the power of death."*

Where had I heard that before? Yeah, I know it's
in the Bible, but I had been told this before and was
almost as embarrassed then as I was right now. Not
long before this, my mom had invited me out to dinner
to talk. After some small talk, she told me this phrase.
She explained to me that in watching the way I was
with Laura, she noticed that I was very mean and that
my jokes were very hurtful. This is now her daughter-
in-law and she hated to see her being hurt by my harsh,

sarcastic sense of humor. Yeah, I knew exactly what God was talking about.

> *"Laura is My princess*
> *and I chose you*
> *to care for her."*

So I tried to change. I tried to control my hurtful comments. But most importantly, I would try to go to Laura and apologize when I knew that I had hurt her. Sadly, this was rare; I still have my pride and this was really tough.

I started listening when she told me of things that hurt her. I wanted her to be okay, but really...I wanted God to see that she was the problem, not me.

We still fought and I was challenged on most all of my decisions. Everything I did seemed to be wrong. I came to the conclusion that if I would involve her in the process, then everything would be fine. I kept hearing from her that all she wanted was to be a part of the decision with me instead of having to just submit to my orders. So I tried, but that was not the answer. She thought it was; I thought it was; but it absolutely didn't change a thing. I was still the bad guy.

It didn't take me long to realize that I wasn't respected, wasn't trusted, wasn't loved; and that realization was a huge blow to me. I could not figure out why she had changed. It hadn't been that long ago when I was that great guy that she wanted to show off to everybody. Now, she didn't like me, didn't respect me and was even mad at me. I thought we were in this together. I thought we were a team. I thought we were both responsible for the mistakes we made.

It was time for drastic measures. It was time to figure this out, once and for all. It was time to involve...the Bible.

Chapter Four
Mine's Broken!

I was reading in Ephesians chapter 5 as I had so many times before. I practically knew it by heart; well...some of it. I loved reading it. It gave me such encouragement that I was right. It says,

> **"Wives, submit to your own husbands** (that was me)**, as to the Lord. For the husband is head of the wife..."**
> **(Ephesians 5:22-23)**

Then it says some other stuff that really didn't keep my interest, and then it says,

> **"...so let the wives be** (subject) **to their own husbands in everything."**
> **(Ephesians 5:24)**

Did you see the "in everything" part? I loved that part. It would just minister to my soul so much. Then God added some extra words and light reading that I kind of skip over to get to the meat. The meat is where it says,

> **"...and let the wife see that she respects her husband."**
> **(Ephesians 5:33)**

Boom!
I could just see the Holy Spirit drop the mic.

I knew that Laura was a good Christian woman. I knew that she would do everything in her power to try to love and respect me. She had to, or burn in hell. Okay, maybe God would forgive her, but she still had to. I also knew that she couldn't make herself love me. As Emily Dickinson put it, "The heart wants what it wants, or else it does not care."

But there was a problem inside of me that I was struggling with. Although I loved what God was saying about the rules that she had to follow, I didn't want forced love. I didn't want her to respect me because the Bible commanded her to, I wanted her to respect me because I was worthy of it, even though I knew I wasn't. I wanted true respect, true honor and true love.

This is when I began to learn a bit about God's love for me and what He wants from me. He doesn't want a puppet or a robot. He wants me to love Him because I want to, not because I have to. He doesn't want to control me or gain my love because He gives me things or keeps me from getting hurt. God wants me to love Him in good times and bad, and that's what I wanted from Laura, no less.

I realized that if this thing was going to work, I was going to have to step up my game. I was going to have to dig deep and really sell this "Love" thing.

I spent the next three years dedicating myself to convincing my wife that I loved her, at least I did in my mind. I did all the right things. Valentine's Day was huge. Our anniversary was like a national holiday. I took every chance I could find to impress her and show her how great a catch I was. I knew that eventually she would just crumble under the weight of my love.

As time went on, I began to see it. It became clearer and clearer. Everything I had been doing for the last three years was having...no effect whatsoever.

I couldn't believe it. This was good stuff I was wasting on a girl who was never going to change. She didn't trust me, she didn't love me, she didn't respect me and I was clueless as to how to fix this thing.

I had this belief that most wives, if not all other wives, were wonderful. I thought my wife was okay, but needed some work. She wasn't awful or even mean and hurtful, just sort of...broken. I can say this because I am the one who broke her.

I knew deep down that I loved her; I just couldn't get her to see or feel it. I was completely stumped. I had never really run up against something that I felt like I couldn't accomplish. I wanted a good marriage, and I wanted that marriage to be with Laura; but maybe I was wrong. I began to have so many thoughts about options and other directions that I could gone. Maybe it would be better for both of us to cut our losses now and move on before we have miserable lives. What I really meant was, maybe it would be better for me. I wasn't really thinking that Laura would find someone that could help fix her problem. After all, if I can't do it, nobody can. I know that sounds pretty arrogant, but that is just how I felt in thinking that I had done everything possible.

However, at the end of every conversation with myself, I knew she was right for me and I was right for her; and knowing that is what kept me from making a bad situation worse. Every time I came close to giving up hope, I would just hang on to the commitment that I made. Our commitment kept us together through some really bad times; but sometimes even that didn't seem to be good enough.

I cried out to God, "Mine's broken!"

I wanted God to know the situation that He had put me in. I wanted Him to see that I had tried everything to make it work. I wanted Him to do a miracle and just "Zap" Laura. I wanted God to fix it.

Then God answered.

I was sitting in bed one night watching TV; well, not really watching, but I had it on for noise. I became overwhelmed with thoughts about my relationship with Laura. I knew that it was God. I knew He was talking to me, and I knew He was not going to let me off easy. All these thoughts kept ending with Him asking me the same question...

"Do you love Laura?"

"Of course I love her. Can't you see what I have been doing for the last three years? I've sacrificed and given. I've paid my dues and done my half of the work. What kind of question is that?"

Without any anger or judgment, I heard Him ask,

> *"What is she worth to you?"*

Without hesitation, I blurted out...

"Everything."

I knew as soon as I said it that I was about to be called out. Sometimes I say things, and even as I am saying the words, I want to stop talking. I want to hold my tongue and just sit and look wise. I usually don't, but I was hoping that the God of the universe, the Alpha and the Omega, the King of kings and Lord of lords would ignore my fake bravado and arrogance. I was hoping that He would just let this one slide by and say, "Good job, son."

He didn't. Instead, He said,

> *"I'm going to teach*
> *you about Love,*
> *then we'll talk again."*

This is when life gets really scary for me. I know I have a good Father and I know He loves me; but often times in my life when I have to learn something, it hurts. I was already tired and didn't want to hurt. I didn't want to learn anything; I just wanted God to fix it.

I was anxious to get this learning started and over with, but I didn't hear anything from Him for a while. Slowly, the fluff parts of Ephesians that I used to avoid started to nag at me. For some unknown reason, I began to pay attention to the "dots." That's what I call the parts I typically skip over in writing or teaching. I grew up seeing so many pastors start their Bible quotes with "...". I didn't really ever realize that those are important parts of the Bible too.

As I sat there actually reading the "dots" of Ephesians, the thought occurred to me that this Apostle Paul character probably took some of this writing into his own hands. This couldn't be God. I loved my wife so I could just skip over this part. Done and done...or so I thought; but these skipped words just wouldn't go away. I began noticing that even the lines that were about my wife had a lot to do with me.

"For the husband is head of the wife, even as Christ is head of the church; and He is the Savior of the body." (Ephesians 5:23)

Then I noticed that there was a whole lot more writing about husbands and their duties than there was about wives. It says,

> **"Husbands, love your wives, just as Christ also loved the church and gave Himself for her, that He might sanctify and cleanse her, with the washing of water by the word, that He might present her to Himself a glorious church, not having spot or wrinkle or any such thing, but that she should be holy and without blemish. So husbands ought to love their own wives as their own bodies; he who loves his wife loves himself. For no one ever hated his own flesh, but nourishes and cherishes it, just as the Lord does the church. For we are members of His body, of His flesh and of His bones. 'For this reason a man shall leave his father and mother and be joined to his wife, and the two shall become one flesh.'" (Ephesians 5:25-31)**

Wait a second...does God think I don't love her like that, 'cause I do... I so do...I really, really do. I loved her like all the love songs I knew. I loved her like all the stupid poems I had to learn in high school English class. I loved her like the rivers run to the sea. I loved her like the birds love to sing; like the mountains high, like the valleys low...I can do this all day.

Just as I was struggling between "What is God saying?" and "Do I really love my wife?" God broke in again.

"What is Love?"

 # Brad's Shorts

See Things My Way

*M*y wife and I have been married for 29 years now, and I wouldn't trade those years for anything. She really is one of the only people from whom I get honest reactions, even when I don't ask her for them.

She is a petite Cuban/Guatemalan lady who towers over her world at four feet eleven and three quarter inches. She will fight anyone who says she is less than five feet, but she is not here as I write this.

As we have grown older, she keeps me in check.
She tells me when I can't lift something.
But I can.
She tells me when my hair is turning gray.

It's actually not.

And she lets me know when my eyes need to be checked.

I can see perfectly.

After a recent discussion about my eyesight, I began to ponder things. I actually did injure my eyes years ago while working on a construction job. It doesn't affect my sight, but I do have scars on my eyes, so they are always red. For 25 years I have thought that someday, when technology gets much better, I would look into having them fixed. Could now be that time?

We recently moved to the Dallas area and options are so much better here than where we lived before, and eye surgery has come a long way.

As I drive up Highway 114, I notice a building off to my right that says "Lasik and Cataract."

Now I'm thinking about it all the time; but do I need Lasik or do I have cataracts. Could it be neither? Could it be both?

I can't just stop in and check. I know these guys are just like mechanics with my car. If I take my car in to my mechanic, he will find something wrong. That's how they make money.

Whatever I do, I'm not letting my wife know that she may have been right. I am still strong enough! My hair is not gray! And I see just fine!

Now driving down Highway 121, I notice a new eye center with a fantastic billboard. It is the kind of billboard with LED lights that are constantly changing. In passing, I notice just enough to see two ads. "Lasik for $469" and "Cataract for $399."

I realize that this price is probably per eye, but even that isn't bad.

I didn't catch the name of the place but I know where it is, so I can always find it; and I was very impressed with the investment in the nice building and signage.

Not long after this, my wife pointed out again my struggle to see clearly. She was wrong, but I could be persuaded to go in and find out what might be done about this scar tissue. I mentioned to her that I found a place I would like to take her.

Driving down the road, I casually mention that I think my eyesight is fine but I am curious about this scar tissue and what could be done about it; but again, there is nothing wrong with my eyesight.

"Really?" she says.

As I pull into the very large clinic, I notice that they are very busy, with lots of cars in the parking lot.

"What are we doing here?" she asks.

"This is the place I was telling you about," I reply.

With excitement in her voice, she asks, "Are you buying me a new car?"

I look up and realize that I am at a very expensive car dealership.

I quickly scan the horizon for that fantastic billboard that I know was here. Found it.

It said, "Lexus $469" and the next sign said "Cadillac $399."

"Uhh...If we can agree that my eyesight is fine, then yes, Sweetie, we are getting you a new car."

Chapter Five
What is Love?

Poems have been penned about it. Songs have been written and rewritten, sung and re-sung about it. It seems like so many of us are trying to express our love in so many ways to show each other how we truly feel. Expressing how I felt was easy. I could just copy so many who have gone before me and use their words, their songs, their feelings. I could even blend some of those expressions together to personalize it a little more.

God had asked me,

"What is love?"

I felt like it was a trick question, but I tried to think of any way I could to describe it. Of course, I defaulted back to what I knew others had done.

I said, "Love is a deep emotion that..."

"No," He said.

"I mean, love is not an emotion, but rather a commitment."

"No," He said.

"Love is a feeling."

"No," He said.

"Love is an intense..."

"No."

"Love is the..."

"Nope."

"It's a..."

"No."

"It's like..."

"Wrong."

I tried to think of every Bible verse I had ever heard about love.

~ 54 ~

"Love is patient..."

"No"

"Love is kind..."

"No"

"Love is..."
"Love is..."
"Love is..."

"No."
"No."
"No."

"I'd like to use a lifeline!"
"Can I phone a friend?"
"Can I get a hint?"
"I don't know."

*"How can you say you Love her
if you don't even know
what Love is?"*

I was stumped. I thought I knew. I thought that I was a man who truly enjoyed love. I like sappy movies with my wife. I like happy endings. I like it when guys go all out to show their wives how they feel. I was beginning to realize that I didn't know Love, I was just a romantic. That was my personality, not necessarily who I actually was, and definitely not Love.

~ 55 ~

I felt like my whole adult life had been a facade. Everything I had tried with Laura was wrong; not bad, just wrong. It was wrong because it had the incorrect goal: I was trying to save a marriage. I was trying to fix Laura. I was trying to do it right. I was trying to not fail. All of these things could be considered good, but not for me and not now.

I wanted to know about Love. I wanted to learn. I wanted to Love my wife. This is when God showed me something that changed my life, forever.

He said,

> *"This is simple, not easy. It is just one word, but it is more complex than anything you will ever know, see or do. The more you understand, the more you realize that you don't understand as much as you thought."*

"I'm ready to understand, or not understand, or...I'm ready to learn. What is Love?

> *"I AM."*

"Yeah, and...."

I was kind of hoping for a little more. Not more than God, but more of a definition. I kept asking and asking.

"What does that mean?"
"What do I do with that?"
"And, by the way, that was two words."
"What is Love?"

He was silent. For some time, I was stuck with this thought in my head...What is Love? I'm a thinker and a contemplator. I like to reason things out. I spent a lot of time trying to figure out what God meant by this. Although I consider myself a thinker, I have to admit that I am not always that quick to come up with the easiest solution; but I finally got to the next step.

I was sitting in my car one day enjoying the radiant heat from the sunshine while I was waiting on Laura for something. I had my Bible in between the seats, and I don't even know why but I grabbed it and opened to 1 John chapter 4. As I sat there reading, it hit me. Like a ton of bricks, it hit me.

Verse 8 says,

"He who does not love does not know God, for God is love."

Then again in verse 16 He says,

"...God is love...."

Has anyone else ever seen this? This is gold! I wanted to run and tell everyone what I had found...the definition of Love. It is so obvious. I can't believe nobody ever told me this. We need billboards, bumper stickers, t-shirts, an entire ad campaign! This is huge! This is fantastic and it is so...easy!

That's when God broke in again.

"It's simple, not easy."

Right...that's what I meant.

"So, now that you know what Love is, how are you going to Love Laura?"

"I'm going to...."
"Well, I'm gonna...."
"I'll probably just...."
"I have absolutely no idea."

"How do I Love you?"

I was flooded with ideas of all the ways that God Loves me, from the job that I have to the air I breathe. I thought of so many things that God has done for me, to me and with me. I've been successful, I've been blessed and I've even been healed: but still, everything came back to the main thought of how God Loves me: He died for me. He rose for me. He was my Savior. He was my King. He was my Everything. Then my thoughts went to anticipating what He was going to say next. I could almost hear His deep voice saying, "Brad, go and do likewise!"

I hadn't really said a word to Him yet; but just as I was finishing that thought, He said,

> **"Great. You know how**
> **I Love you,**
> **now how are you going**
> **to Love Laura?"**

"Well, I'm still not sure. Am I supposed to be her savior? Am I supposed to die for her? I'm willing to, you know, but I hope it doesn't come to that. I mean, if I die just so she can be Loved, that would stink. I would be dead and she could now Love me...but I would be dead. That can't be right. Is it? It's not...is it?"

Nothing but silence. I went days wondering what He really meant by this. My mind would just not allow that to be true. Love has to be more than just giving up one's life for another; and it has to be more than just being willing to. There has to be a way to learn to Love Laura and I was finally getting to the point that I really wanted to.

As time went on, I began to see Laura in a different light. I don't know how, and I don't even know what changed. I just had a feeling about her that I hadn't felt since before we were married. I wanted to be with her. I wanted to be her friend. I wanted her to be happy. I wasn't trying to save a marriage or to avoid a divorce. I wasn't trying to win a game or achieve a trophy. I was pursuing a woman that I really wanted to Love.

~ 59 ~

The thought crossed my mind that God had finally done it. He had given me Love for Laura and now everything was going to be great, just like I expected. Ohhh...He is such a good God. He was right, this was simple. But actually, it was also pretty easy. He is a good God.

I was so excited. I was finally on the right track and life was good...or about to be, just as soon as Laura realizes that God did this great miracle. All I had to do was to be willing to die for her and that was the key to Love. It made sense: Jesus died for me and showed me His Love, so....

But things didn't really improve. All my actions done in "Love" were judged as fake, contrived, or just gimmicks. Laura wasn't swayed at all. I didn't understand. This was supposed to work. I explained to her that "God had said..." so she has to get okay with it; but no...no change, no trust, no respect.

I was so discouraged. I still looked at her with this new "Love" in my heart, but it just wasn't working. She was supposed to get giddy at the sight of me. She was supposed to blush when I wink at her. She was supposed to fall in Love with me. I had no idea what I was doing wrong. I knew it had to be me, because God had fixed it. He gave me this new "Love" for her and I still couldn't make it work.

Finally, I couldn't stand it any longer. I cried out to God and begged Him to fix it again. I told God that I was sorry and that I would like another chance. I wanted to start again.

He answered me in a very curious way that I was not expecting.

"You haven't started yet."

"What do you mean I haven't started yet?"

I couldn't believe it. God hadn't seen any of the work that I had been putting in. How could He have missed it?

"I've been trying to Love her and now I look at her with Your eyes and I Love her with your Love. You did it. You gave me a heart for Laura and I have fallen in Love with her all over again."

I went on as I usually do, having a one-sided conversation with God, in which I tell Him exactly what I think He's trying to teach me. He usually waits until I'm done and have gone down some stupid rabbit trail before He says anything. This time was no different. I continued to talk myself into what I think would be best. I find that it helps to really believe it if I imagine God's answers in a deep voice. It doesn't make them any truer, but at least they feel more real.

"...so I guess what You're saying is for me to start Loving her and she will eventually fall in Love with me? That sounds easy enough."

Then I heard those three little words again,

"Simple, not easy...."

Chapter Six
Simple, Not Easy

My first big business deal was one in which I was purchasing a small company and all of its assets for $100,000. I had seen the numbers and I knew what the business brought in. I thought there was potential to increase market share. I felt like it was a good deal, but it was my first big deal. I was risking everything that I had already built. To some, it wasn't much; but to Laura and me, it was a huge deal. I didn't have the money and was borrowing it from the bank. I still remember that morning. There were four of us in the conference room: my banker, the two guys from whom I was buying, and me. I had the pen in my hand, and as the papers were passed to me, I paused.

Just sign my name. I had signed my name so many times before. Place the pen about an inch above the bottom line and begin moving it downward and then up again. I know how to sign my name; it's simple.

It was simple, but not easy. So many times in my life, I have come across this same problem: decisions that are hard to make, steps that are hard to take, things that are hard to tell someone. Even the whole idea of faith is simple, but not easy. Every time I come up against this problem, I remember how God first taught me this principle as I was learning to Love Laura.

I was lying in my bed one night in the quiet, in the dark. We had been married just over four years—not happily married, just married.

I could hear her breathing as she was lying next to me. It wasn't steady breathing so I knew she was still awake. We had just finished a fight, or rather not finished it, and were now ignoring each other. It was just life as usual.

In the silence of the night, I heard God.

"Tell her,
Goodnight Gorgeous."

"Wait...what?"
"Goodnight Gorgeous...?"
"Is that all?"

I said it in my head over and over. It just sounded fake...and then it began sounding weird because I was saying it over and over. I mentally tried it with a British accent and then with a Texas drawl. I heard it so clear with a thick New York accent and finally just my normal voice. Then I had to question if He had said

"Beautiful" or "Gorgeous." The word "Beautiful" flows much better in this situation and I think it might be a little more convincing to her if I say it that way. Then I just wondered if I was making all of this up. Maybe I'm supposed to add, "Rest well," or "Sleep tight. Don't let the bed bugs bite" or "I love you." Oh...that's the one. "I love you." Yeah, that would be good.

Okay, so...I will say the thing God said to say and then add a short, soft, heartfelt, "I love you." I continued practicing it in my head. Oh man, she is going to melt. God and I make a pretty good team.

Then it started to weigh on me that God shouldn't really need my help in this. He knows her better than I do. Why isn't He doing more? Why isn't He saying more? Was He sure that this was all I was needing to say?

Without making a noise, I asked God why. I asked what He meant. I asked Him to repeat it.

Nothing.

As I laid there in the quiet, I carefully talked myself out of this silly line of thinking and tried to go to sleep. But I couldn't stop thinking about how much I wanted to trust God. He said it was simple, not easy. This couldn't be from Him because this is pretty easy. Easy...and yet I can't bring myself to say it.

Then the thought struck me. What if this was the proverbial straw that broke the camel's back? What if this changes everything? What if I say these two simple words and she finally realizes how much I Love her and she begins to trust me again? All these questions came flooding in. This could be the night that we look back on and point to saying, "That was when it all changed." I had to mentally prepare myself for the huge changes about to happen. I was so excited and now I couldn't wait to say these two words.

I broke the silence of the night and said in a soft voice, holding back all my enthusiasm so I didn't sound like an idiot,

"Goodnight Gorgeous."

That was it. It happened. I was ready for the rush of emotion that was about to flood in. Then I heard her break her breathing pattern and say...

"Goodnight."

Wait. That was it? What about the rest. Wasn't she listening to God? I was confused. I had really built this thing up into a huge fix and that was kind of a let-down. In fact, it was very anti-climactic. So I waited. God had to have more. Somewhere in the night, as I was waiting for the next directive, I fell asleep.

The next night I was already in bed when she came into the room. She climbed into bed talking to me about one of her friends. I couldn't wait for her to lie down and stop talking so I could see if God had a plan for the night. We talked for another fifteen minutes before silence overtook us. I laid there trying to hear God and the next step. I wondered what He was going to have me tell her.

Then, all of a sudden, like a lightning bolt splitting the dark, I heard a word.

"Goodnight"

But it wasn't from God. It was Laura. This was not unusual, but I was waiting for God, not Laura.

I flippantly said goodnight and continued in my quiet quest for the right word to break her hard outer shell.

One minute turned into two and then into five. I watched the red lights of the alarm clock slowly change. Ten minutes, eleven, and twelve...I heard her breathing get steady. She was falling asleep and God was going to miss His chance.

> ***"Tell her,***
> ***Goodnight Gorgeous."***

This time I didn't even hesitate. I knew my window was short.

"Goodnight Gorgeous."

"Goodnight," was the soft sound that came back my direction.

Again...? Maybe she isn't really hearing me. I'm speaking the words that God is giving me. Maybe if God got here a little sooner this might work. Maybe my tone is off. Maybe I need more inflection in my voice. I dozed off wondering why this wasn't working.

The next day as I woke up, I noticed that she was already up and out of bed. I laid there asking God what was going on. All I could think about was the fact that this isn't working.

I spent the day wondering if I was doing it wrong, saying it wrong, or hearing it wrong. I watched Laura carefully. I knew that she had free will and I thought maybe she was just resisting God. Isn't that great? I married the one woman on the planet that is able to resist God. I needed God to be stronger. I needed God to reach her. I needed God to heal my marriage.

I continued all day long asking God to show me what was wrong. Why wasn't this working? I didn't hear anything from Him.

That night, as I went to bed, I prayed that God would do something great. Tell me, show me, even do it for me, but please let this be the night that things change. As the lights went out and the silence arrived, nothing happened. What was actually only about twenty minutes seemed like hours. But finally, I heard Him again.

"Tell her,
Goodnight Gorgeous."

"Yeah, that's not really working. Have You got anything else in that playbook, 'cause she's already seen that one."

I waited and waited and waited. I had almost decided that I was not actually hearing God and was just making this up; and then...lying there in the dark, I was flooded with a huge feeling of Love for my wife. I wanted to Love her. I wanted her to be happy, but even more than that, I wanted her to know that she was beautiful.

It was on that night that God showed me how beautiful my wife truly was.

"Goodnight Gorgeous."

 **Brad's Shorts**

A New Restaurant Just Opened...

*M**y wife is a high-school science teacher who loves her job. She teaches in another city not too far away but not exactly close. In addition to wanting to be there early and stay late, she also has a bit of a drive, which doesn't leave much time in the evenings for eating out; so we typically plan ahead to eat out, shop and do most all of our entertaining on weekends.*

One morning before she left for work, she mentioned a new restaurant that she wanted to try.

"Would you like to go to Señor Wok next Saturday? It's in Denton."

Planning two weeks ahead was not usual, but I knew our current upcoming weekend was already full. Not thinking much of it, I replied, "Sounds great."

Then I began thinking about the restaurant... Señor Wok. This may be the perfect combination of Chinese and Mexican food. I quickly remembered all the curious restaurants that I have seen.

There was the coffee and mail center,

"Sip and Ship,"

the coin-op laundromat and burger joint,

"Suds and Grub,"

and all the Vietnamese soup places like

"Lu Pho" and "Pho Nhi"

(the Pho is pronounced fuh and the Nhi is pronounced knee).

And I'll never forget the

"Ann Thai Kitchen."

Yes, I laugh at people, but this one intrigued me. I began to think of the possibilities.

Sweet-n-Sour Enchiladas!?!

Stir-fried burritos!?!

General Tso's Tacos!?!

With almost no time passing in our conversation, I mentioned to my beautiful wife, "That really sounds good."

"Great! Then it's a date," and off to work she went.

As I was getting ready for work I began to daydream in Chinese/Mexican culinary drama.

"Kung Pao Chorizo."

"Moo Goo Gorditas."

All week I was distracted by the idea of this place. On Sunday, while relaxing in the living room, I reached a stopping point in my thoughts.

"Chimichangas!"

Knowing how funny I consider myself to be, I casually asked my wife,

"Are Chimichangas Mexican or Chinese?"

Realizing that this is one of my stupid questions, she answered that they are Tex-Mex.

"But...," I said.

Just then her phone rang. It was her sister-in-law, Kayla. She'll be on the phone for a while, but I really wanted to talk about this. I see some real promise in this Chinese/Mexican dish, and they would not even need to change the name.

Saturday came and we enjoyed our usual coffee time in the morning. She went to get ready to go and came out looking absolutely stunning in her dress.

She casually said to me, "Are you going to get ready?"

I was wearing my jeans, boots and a nice-enough polo shirt, but I'm pretty quick on the uptake and was able to see that she wanted this to be a "nice date." I quickly ran to my closet and changed into my slacks and dress shoes, and a really nice dress shirt that she bought for me not too long ago.

"Do I need a sport coat?" I yelled out to her.

"Not at all." she yelled back.

We headed out to the garage and she mentioned that she had forgotten something. When she turned to go back inside the house, I quickly grabbed my detail towels and spray, and wiped down the outside of her

BMW. I had it looking great. I grabbed the leather spray and squirted it twice into the trunk; just the right amount of scent.

"Perfect!" I said out loud.

She came back out and I was holding her door open for her. I closed the door behind her and climbed into the driver's seat.

As we were headed to Denton, a town about 15 minutes away, I asked how she heard about this place.

"They told us at school where it is," she said.

Noticing her really gorgeous legs and high heels I said, "I didn't realize it was going to be this nice a place."

"It's not the place that's nice, it's the purpose," she said.

Curious and a little confused, I said, "What is the purpose?"

"...same as last year. It should only last about two hours," she remarked.

"Last year? I thought this was a new place," I said with fear and trembling beginning to show through in my voice.

"What are you talking about?" she questioned.

"Aren't we going to Señor Wok?" I begged.

She laughed out loud.

"We are going to SENIOR WALK! Commencement. High School Graduation."

I actually teared up.

Chapter Seven
Brace for Impact

The tee box on the ninth hole where I play golf is lined up perfectly down the side of an oncoming hole. If I slice, which is something I don't often admit to, I can easily end up on the sixth fairway. People playing there can get really upset when they hear you yell, "FORE." They know that a ball from the other tee box is coming into their area. Their initial reaction is usually to duck and cover their head, followed shortly after by their attempt to look up and find the incoming ball. I'm good enough with my driver off the tee box to put it right in the middle of the set up for their second shot. Although I appreciate their concern, I usually try to assure them that it is no reason to get upset. I can easily course correct and still make par; but for some reason they still don't like it. Golfers just don't like being startled like that.

This is much like a time when I was flying into Las Vegas on a budget airline. As we began our descent, the pilot came on the intercom and stated that they are struggling with cross-winds and that the landing might be pretty bumpy. As we made our approach, the plane sped up and gained altitude again. The pilot came on again and said that things are a little more difficult than originally thought and they are going to have to try again. The plane came back around, and just as we were about to touchdown, the pilot came on one more time and said, "BRACE FOR IMPACT."

You never want to hear those words while on a plane. Even if you have never heard that before, you know what it means.

The plane landed swaying back and forth. Somehow that pilot was able to steady up and get the plane to the terminal without any damage...to the plane or, more importantly, to me. Maybe it needed to be said or maybe he jumped the gun, but in my mind it only meant one thing...this is about to hurt.

That's exactly where I was with God. Lying there in bed, in the dark, in the silence, I began to realize what He meant by, "not easy."

I knew He had so much more to teach me and now I felt like I was finally ready to learn. I knew that what I was about to learn is something that I probably should have known and been doing all along.

I tend to learn things by experience. I wish I could just take somebody's opinion and advice, but I know that I often need to "find out for myself." Although this is a great way to learn something deeply so as to reduce chances of forgetting, it is also a very hard way to learn. It usually costs more: more time, more money and more energy, and it usually causes more pain. God was about to teach me how to Love my wife; which meant, in my mind at least, that this was going to hurt...Brace for Impact.

As I laid there with Laura sleeping next to me, I became genuinely sorry. I wasn't sorry for my sin, my mistakes or anything I had done. I knew that I was already forgiven for those things. This was different. I wasn't sorry for my actions, I was sorry for the results of my actions, or inactions. I was deeply sorry for what Laura had gone through because of me. She didn't deserve to be treated the way I treated her. She didn't deserve to be hurt by some punk kid that thought he was pretty cool. She was my gift from God. She was His little girl and she was definitely His Princess. I wasn't even fearful that He was mad at me, just regretful that Laura had not been truly Loved by me. I realized that all my love tricks were just that...tricks. Tricks to make her yield to me, tricks to make her love me and tricks to win; but they were all tricks nonetheless. But now I really wanted her to know Love, to feel Love and to be Loved. The impact of all of this hurt in a way I never expected.

I dozed off somewhere in the night and when I woke the next morning, Laura was already up and out of bed. I knew that something was different. I walked around the house looking and found her in my daughter's room. Still in her pajamas with her hair undone and no make-up, she was the most beautiful thing I had ever seen. I stood in the doorway staring and wondering how to make this feeling last.

Later that day, I began asking God to teach me.

"I'm truly ready this time. I want to know how to treat my wife, how to take care of her, and especially how to Love her so that she feels Loved."

But I heard nothing. I resigned myself to the fact that God was going to teach me when He thought I was ready; so I was going to have to wait.

That night climbing into bed, I had a revelation. I should just continue what God last told me until He changes the plan. Wow! What a concept. Do what God says until He says stop. Yeah, I'm quick that way.

So I did.

After the lights went out and all the talking was done, I waited about thirty seconds. Then I quietly said,

"Goodnight Gorgeous."

The reply came back,
"Goodnight."

Days went by and I continued to end each night with a simple phrase...Goodnight Gorgeous. I just assumed that after a few nights, God would lead me to the next step. I was bound and determined not to give up and not to quit until I heard from God. Every night ended the same way,

"Goodnight Gorgeous."

"Goodnight."

But it wasn't long before I realized that nothing was changing and God wasn't saying or doing anything. How long was this monotonous situation going to go on? I began calling out to God with frustration and annoyance. After all, I knew that the God of the Universe could easily fix this marriage; and I knew that He would, of course, want us to have a good marriage. Why didn't He just put Love in me and put respect in her? But He didn't. He didn't fix it and He didn't tell me why. I kept asking, but heard nothing. This went on for weeks.

"Goodnight Gorgeous."

"Goodnight."

"Goodnight Gorgeous."

"Goodnight."

"Goodnight Gorgeous."

"Goodnight."

Finally, one night, we were lying in bed, the air was still, the night was quiet and there was a wonderful glow from the moon shining in through our window and pouring over Laura's auburn hair. She was facing away from me, which was pretty normal.

"Goodnight Gorgeous."

I said it softly but there was no reply. I spoke a little louder but still tried to make it sound as loving as I could.

"Goodnight Gorgeous."

Again, there was no answer. I had waited too long. I missed my chance. Not only was it not having the miraculous effect that it was supposed to have on my wife, but now she didn't even hear it.

I sat there frustrated and unable to sleep, asking God what was going on. I knew He wasn't going to answer, but I asked anyway. I knew Laura wasn't going to respect me until she trusted me. I was trying so hard to make up for the pain I had caused; and I felt that, for the most part, I was pretty much almost trustworthy. The truth was that I knew I wasn't trustworthy. I also knew that I couldn't ever be perfect, so God had to have a plan for people like me. There had to be a way for me to reach my wife. I needed to get her to trust me, but everything I was trying wasn't working.

Then He answered. Sitting in the dark room looking out at the beautiful moon over the rooftop of the house next door, I began hearing from God again.

"Why do you trust Me?"

Chapter Eight
Trust Me

I'm not sure who came up with the idea, and I'm not sure who came up with the variances on the idea, but I don't like it. I'm talking about the "Trust Fall." Sales teams and business groups all over have adopted it as a means to get people to work as a team; to get them to gel; to basically establish trust.

The "Trust Fall" is a situation in which one person, either blindfolded or eyes shut, falls and trusts that the other members of the group will catch them before they hit the ground. Variations have come along, such as one person with feet planted firmly in the middle of a circle of others as they begin to push that person back and forth. One variation calls for the blindfolded person to fall forward while everybody else is positioned closer to the ground in order to allow the fear of falling to really set in before they are caught. Then there is my favorite: a platform built about 4-5 feet up in the air with a person falling backward off the platform into the arms of people who promise to catch him. This is the mutation of the "Trust Fall" that I was exposed to as a teenager one year at summer camp. We each had to take turns falling off of the platform. There was just one problem...I know that these people are not going to catch me. Sure, they say they will, and sure, they have worked with me to catch each other; but I am not like them. I am much bigger than your average teenager...and I'm really too tall to qualify for this...and my shoes are not made for this...and I'm pretty sure that red-headed guy doesn't even like me. Yeah, he's definitely going to drop me. Is this even legal? Where's OSHA?

When I was catching others, I would do everything I could to catch the falling person; but I know that nobody takes this job as seriously as I do.

Finally, I decided to try it; not because I trusted them, but because I had determined in my head that if I hit the ground perfectly horizontal, it would spread out the impact to a larger area, and therefore would not hurt near as much. I backed up to the edge of the platform and closed my eyes. I lifted my arms and crossed them over my chest. I was ready to fall. I went through the procedure:

"Ready?" I asked very loudly.

"Ready," was the response I heard from a crowd of people that were assuring me that they were ready to let me hit the ground.

"Falling," I said as I leaned back.

The feeling was exhilarating and terrifying all at once. I'm sure that is exactly what the guy who came up with this idea wanted me to feel. As I plummeted to the earth and certain death, I tried to garner up the belief that these people were actually going to catch me. But I quickly realized that I could not remember a single strong guy in the group: the kind of guy that could catch me. It was all girls, and small girls at that. Even that red-headed guy who wants me dead was nowhere to be found. I mentally went around the circle and pictured everybody and where they were positioned to do their part. There was the girl who looked like Olive Oil from the Popeye cartoons, skinny arms and all; there were the two twin baby girls who couldn't be more than three months old; and there was Marge Milligan, my grandmother's 78-year-old next-door neighbor. Why she was here, I have no idea; but no...no strong guys to catch me. So I did what any normal person who was plummeting to their death at 32 feet per second per second would do...I panicked. I removed my arms from their appropriate position on my chest and began flailing them about to grab anything I could on my way down. The back of my right hand found something solid. It was the face of 15-year-old Terry McNab. I have no idea how she got there, because she was not in my mental line-up. She must have slipped in at the last minute in between the two twin babies. Needless to say, the immense pain of the black eye I gave to Terry took precedent over catching anyone falling from over 48 inches up in the air. (I expressed it that way because 48 sounds much bigger than 4. However, I now realize that inches sound incredibly smaller than feet. The point is that I was high up and I could have been killed.)

The group almost completely caught me; but in my book, "almost completely caught me" means they dropped me. My tailbone hit the ground causing a loud thud that people in nearby Cloudcroft, New Mexico were able to hear. Everybody in the group had caught a piece of my body; everybody except Terry McNab. She was positioned right about where my waist should have been caught...and there she sat, covering her eye and crying. Didn't she know that she had a responsibility to catch me? She should have been prepared for anything. Thinking back even now, I'm not sure I ever received an apology from her. So yeah, I have trust issues.

However, those trust issues never seemed to carry over to my relationship with God. I have always known that I could trust Him. On that night, sitting in the dark room looking out at the beautiful moon over the rooftop of the house next door, God asked me,

"Why do you trust Me?"

"I don't know, Lord. I just do."

"Why?"

I felt like I was taking a test that I knew I was going to fail. I tried so hard to figure out why I trusted God, but I ended up saying the first thing that came to my mind.

"...because You Love me.
You have never stopped Loving me.
Even when I didn't Love You back, You...."

As I was saying it, I realized what He was showing me. I trusted Him because He has always Loved me. He had never failed me. Even though He has always been trustworthy, He allowed me to learn to trust Him. I was expecting Laura to trust me immediately; but unlike God, I had already broken her trust. Laura was going to have to learn to trust me and I now realized that this was going to take some time.

"Goodnight Gorgeous."

"Goodnight."

"Goodnight Gorgeous."

"Goodnight."

Night after night, week after week this just continued. It became a very normal thing for us. I actually stopped expecting a different response. I just assumed that God would do it in His time.

"Goodnight Gorgeous."

"Goodnight."

Over time other things began to change as well. Laura and I began to try and have date nights. It was such a struggle. We would plan an evening and go out to dinner, at which time we would sit across from each other and not talk; but at least we were moving forward. Laura wanted a better marriage as well; she just had no idea how bad I had hurt her or how much she was burying deep inside.

"Goodnight Gorgeous."

"Goodnight."

While God was teaching me patience and perseverance, He was also teaching Laura so much. She wanted to respect me, but there is something in a person that will not let them lie to themselves. Laura couldn't respect me because she didn't respect me. I knew it was a command from God and she did too, but all she could do was to try and show me respect by acting respectful in spite of how she felt. And as much as I appreciated the effort, I didn't want it. I wanted real respect, not lip service. Don't get me wrong, being respected by my wife in public was better than not being respected, even if it was fake. I used to care so much about how other people saw us and demanded her respect in public. I was okay with her feeling any way she wanted as long as it didn't show to the outside world; but now I was over most of that. I cared much less about how other people saw us and was truly beginning to care more about how Laura saw me.

"Goodnight Gorgeous."

"Goodnight."

I tried to fix the little things in my own way. I would go to work and come home, and never think about calling her during the day. One day she mentioned the fact that I don't ever think about calling her; so I came up with a great plan.

At this time in my life I carried a pager. A pager is something that we thought was so cool long before we had cell phones. If anybody called my number, it would send me an alert and I could call to get my message or simply call them back...and they didn't give these things out to just anybody. You had to have at least $5 per month to pay for the service. I had $5, so I got to walk around with a little black box clipped to my hip. I was so cool.

I was able to have my pager alert me every weekday at 10 AM, 2 PM and 4 PM. When the alert came through to my pager, it said "Call Laura."

It worked flawlessly. All of a sudden, I was calling my wife three times a day just to say, "Hi."

I really earned points for this until the third Monday in February. I had taken the day off to spend with my family. We were driving down the road and I had set my pager on the dashboard. Sure enough, at 10 AM, the alert came through. For a half-second I wondered who it could be. Then Laura reached up to check it for me. As she grabbed the pager and turned it upward to read the message, I realized who was paging me.

"Call Laura," she said. "Why does your pager say to call me?"

I could not come up with a good reason and as I tried to think, she realized what the situation was.

All the great spontaneous acts of love had just been undone by Presidents' Day. This was a huge setback. I was trying to win her trust and I just presented her with a situation showing that I am still not trustworthy. I was trying to do the act without having to really be sincere. The cost of this blunder was huge, but still the nightly routine continued.

"Goodnight Gorgeous."

"Goodnight."

I stopped the pager from sending me these alerts and just decided to forego all efforts of calling my wife during the workday. I wasn't sure how else I could remind myself to call her without being a jerk for needing to remind myself to call her. That's when a very interesting thing happened: I was used to my pager going off three times a day and thought about it quite often...so I called my wife.

Of course the reception on the other end was not appreciated and I had a lot of make-up work to do. Laura eventually realized that I was now calling her because I wanted to and not because I was being told to. My pager alerting me three times a day for months trained me to think differently. My thinking trained me to act differently and my actions eventually began to break down the wall of problems I had built in my marriage.

And I always continued,

"Goodnight Gorgeous."

"Goodnight," was always the reply.

 **Brad's Shorts**

Chocolate Turtles

*L*ast week, my wife and I spent the day shopping in a nearby town. It was, as she says, "Quaint."

I don't think I would really know quaint from whatever the opposite of quaint is, but I did enjoy the day walking with my beautiful wife up Main Street into all the shops.

We went into one shop about halfway up Main Street, which was apparently a gift shop of some kind. I know this because as soon as we entered, I saw all the ridiculous things that "Artsy" people love to give as gifts, like the 2-foot high statue of a frog standing up that I am supposed to place in my yard. Why? I have no idea. There were so many other items that I didn't understand as well.

My wife went crazy, like a kid in a candy store, browsing through all the decor, coffees and sweets this place had to offer. I, on the other hand, actually wished we were in a real candy store. Even as I sit here and recall this story, I am daydreaming of soft licorice, cherry sours and wax root beer bottles. I would even be fine with some of those square things that are so hard to describe that nobody ever knows what you're talking about.

I soon became distracted by a section of the shelf on the side wall full of 4-inch ceramic bathroom tiles that were engraved with different sayings; some cute, some not so much. I began to search for all the ones that I would like to put into the wall in our bathroom.

> *You can do it!*
> *If you don't slip in the shower.*

and

> *Give cupcakes to all your friends.*
> *It will make you look thinner.*

As I was browsing through all these tiles, I heard my wife call out,

"Hey, they have chocolate turtles!"

I have to be honest; I was only half-listening. I can say this because she knows that I only ever half-listen.

"Great," I replied.

But it wasn't great. I don't know a whole lot about decorating, but I know that my wife has themes in our house: the western theme of our guest room; the golf theme of my office (I chose that one!); the expensive picture frames on the mantle that have no pictures in them (I still don't understand that one.); even the flowers that I gave her twenty years ago, that she set out to dry for weeks, tied them together and hung them upside down by a hook on the wall.

Inside or outside, I know we do not have a turtle theme. Now I was worried. How much is this new theme going to cost me?

"Wait, what for?" I asked out loud, so that all the people in the store can hear. This way they know that I think some of their decorating ideas should be scrapped.

"...for after dinner," she replied.

It was then that it dawned on me what "Chocolate Turtles" really are: pecans, caramel and chocolate. I literally began to salivate right there. How cool is this? I wanted candy...God gives me candy. This is so wonderful and...Ohhhhhhh crud! Chocolates after dinner only meant one thing...we're having company.

Trying to act cool in front of a store full of people, I said, "Sounds great. Who's coming over tonight?"

"Nobody, just us," she said very non-chalantly.

"Yes!" I exclaimed, mostly to my self, while grabbing air from above my head in my fist and pulling it down to my chest.

As we got back in the car, I realized that it was only 11 AM. I wasn't going to make it 'til dinner.

In a calm, half-joking voice I said, "We should break open that package now."

"What do you mean?" she responded.

I knew that there was no way I was going to get that candy before tonight, but I had to try.

"I think we should..." then her phone rang. It was her mom. There goes my chance.

The rest of the day was filled with stops at different shops and stores. My mind couldn't stop. I could not remember the last time my wife bought me candy for after dinner. I had to wonder: was my son coming home for the weekend? Were we celebrating something that I didn't remember?

Then it hit me! It was our anniversary! I can't believe I forgot that. No. Wait. I already forgot that one about a month ago. What could it be? I forced myself to calm down. I knew when we arrived at home she would still be occupied with her mom, and I could get a "snack." But, I also knew she would hide the candy, knowing that I would do just that...and she did.

At dinner that evening, I pretended not to care. After dinner, we had our normal coffee time and it was so good. I knew that any minute now she would present the long-anticipated chocolates and I would soon be in "turtle heaven."

After a moment she came in, sat down and began to sip her coffee.

"Really good coffee," I said.

"I know, I just love it," she replied with her eyes slightly closed and a smile on her face.

She is driving me crazy.

"Aren't you forgetting something?" I asked.

"What?" she questioned.

Ok! This isn't funny. I've been waiting all day and I've been good...and she knows it.

"THE CHOCOLATE TURTLES!" I exclaimed.

"What?" she questioned, beginning to smile.

"It's Chocolate Turtle flavored coffee," she said, now laughing out loud.

"Uhh...yeah, I know. I was just joking," I said, trying to hide my confusion and disappointment.

Chapter Nine
Life Goes On.

When I was in my 5th grade homeroom class one morning, it was announced over the intercom system that football tryouts would be held after school. I had never played football, except for running around in my front yard pretending to be Drew Pearson. I threw the ball to myself and, of course, caught it one-handed, out maneuvered my dogs and ran all the way to the pecan trees for a touchdown. Yeah, I was really that good.

All the cool guys in class were talking about tryouts; any guy who didn't show up would obviously be an outcast. Then Richard Holland from two seats over to my right turned and asked,

"Hey Brad, are you going to tryouts?"

I casually responded with,

"Yeah,...probably."

I was so cool.

So I showed up at tryouts.

We ran, sprinted and caught the ball. Most guys didn't catch it, but I did; well, almost. We did push-ups, sit-ups and squats. At the end of the afternoon, I was informed that there was not enough room on the team for me but they could recommend another team that needed players. I knew what they meant:

"Hey kid, you stink!"

"Another team?"

"Another team" always ends up being the last in the league. "Another team" is the one that never wins and is usually led by a great volunteer woman like my mom, because they need a coach. It never works out like it does in Hollywood, where the underdogs that know nothing about how to play end up winning everything.

I wasn't doing that.

I went home defeated. I sulked around for a while until my dad called me in and asked about my day. I told him how great I did and how fast I ran. I told him that I didn't think the coaches were watching me and that I should've made the team.

He just snickered and said,

"Well, life goes on."

Life goes on? Are you kidding me? This was catastrophic. My whole future was resting on this. I had been planning on making the Zachary White Elementary School 5th grade football team for almost five or six hours. This was not something I took lightly. This was huge.

But life did go on. Here I was ten years later, married with a child.

I was okay.

I had survived childhood, my teens and young adulthood. I'm sure I will survive this point in my marriage. I know that one day I will be happily married and even more importantly, Laura will be happily married. I continued every night as the lights went out and the air got still,

"Goodnight Gorgeous."

"Goodnight," was always the reply.

Life went on. We got involved in church and everything looked good from the outside. We made friends and started a small group that would meet in our house. For some reason, when you are the facilitator, people think that you have got your whole life together. We would hear from other couples about their marriages and how they fight and we'd actually be thankful that we were not them. We rarely opened up to others about our relationship. There were a few times that I really felt like Laura needed to talk to someone, so we agreed that she could discuss anything she wanted to with a few key people, but we were careful with everybody else. Not just because I didn't want everybody to know my business, or that I was worried about what they would think, but I had a bigger reason for not opening up.

People love to help. People love to give advice. I know...it was one of my spiritual gifts for years. I could look at you and tell you everything that I thought was wrong with you and everything you needed to do to "fix it." It made me feel good to help others. "No thanks needed...it's my pleasure."

Once I realized that I was this way, I couldn't stand it. I decided to try to mind my own business until I was asked.

Laura would often ask me if I thought it might be beneficial to talk to others about our problems...I always objected. I just didn't find too many people that I thought had the marriage that I wanted. I didn't see many marriages that I wanted to learn from. I saw how people would talk to and treat each other when they weren't at church, and I didn't like it. I definitely wasn't going to try to replicate that...and I really wasn't interested in hearing what they thought might be wrong with my marriage. So we kept it all in, and life went on.

"Goodnight Gorgeous."

"Goodnight."

Our businesses were growing and our children were in school, and we were experiencing "real life." We bought a house and some cars. We traveled a bit, some to Europe but mostly around the United States; usually to visit family because it was much cheaper.

I would still continually cry out to God and ask for better for my marriage, but I never heard anything. I know Laura was doing the same. Life was going on and we were not happy. We weren't unhappy, but really felt like there has got to be more to Love and marriage than this. The worst part for me was knowing that Laura was not happy and not being able to fix it. I hated it. It was lukewarm. It was boring. It was milk toast...sustenance, but disgusting.

Why wasn't God doing anything? I couldn't see the repairs. I couldn't feel anything getting better, but I continued to tell my wife, every night,

"Goodnight Gorgeous."

"Goodnight."

I mostly did it out of habit, but I think it became a part of who I was. "Gorgeous" became one of the pet names I would call her...not just at night, but all the time: Gorgeous, Beautiful, Love. But my favorite, my default pet name for Laura was always Gorgeous.

I began to see her this way. I began to think of her as so beautiful, so sexy and so gorgeous. I couldn't really put a date and time on when it happened, but little by little I began to fall in love with her more and more. I began wanting to hurry home from work to see her, and really looking forward to being with her. I began to love my weekends more than building my business. I loved taking her places and even began to like shopping.

I remember looking back and wondering when all this started. When did I change? When did I start feeling this? And of course, I always wondered if Laura was feeling different too.

"Goodnight Gorgeous."

"Goodnight."

Chapter Ten
Reaching The Sink

My mom can find anything on sale. She is the most amazing shopper I have ever seen. When we would go to Gibson's or Pic & Save, the managers used to cringe when they saw her coming. She found things on sale that they didn't even know they had: like the lime green sport coat with matching pants that she bought for her nine-year-old son to wear on Mother's Day; or the blue denim jeans that fit her son perfectly in the waist but were seven sizes too big in the length and therefore had to be hemmed. I was the only kid at school that had hems on my jeans that went up to my knees.

But my favorite purchases that my mom would make were always the shoes. She found deals on shoes that could not be passed up, whether they fit or not. I always had shoes up on a shelf in my closet, usually size 11 or higher. I actually now wear a size 11 and I often think it is because God just got tired of arguing with my mom. She bought the shoes and they were going to fit...period.

I wonder sometimes: when did I officially fit into those shoes? When she bought the shoes, I always got to see them and then they were returned to the box and placed up on the shelf for a later time when they would fit, sometimes years later. But when did I reach the day that those shoes from up on the shelf actually fit? At some random time during the school year when my current shoes were worn out and the rubber sole was separating from the "leather" style fabric, my mom would reach up into the closet and pull down the next set. I knew they would be too big, but somehow they always fit.

This was much like the way we, as children, would one day reach the faucet at the bathroom sink. We couldn't reach it...we couldn't reach it...and then one day we are washing our hands and brushing our teeth as if we had always been doing it this way. I was never really sure what day or time my children were able to completely reach the handles and turn the water on and off. It is just how they grew: very, very slowly.

This is how things were for Laura and me. We just went on with life and things began to get better and better. Yes, I was trying to be a better husband and I know she was trying to be a better wife, but we both knew that we didn't want to just be "better" to each other.

I began to appreciate the things that Laura did for me; everything from cooking dinner to keeping my books at the office. She was truly incredible. We would still fight and argue, but our battles began to look and feel different. They just weren't as mean as they used to be.

I had still not heard any change from God in the plan or strategy, so I continued on with what I knew to do. I was probably doing it wrong and it had been so long now that I figured God would eventually break in and tell me how to do it right...but for now, I just kept moving forward. Every night, I would wait until the discussion was over and she was ready to sleep. I would wait about 30 seconds after the last word was said, and I would pierce the silence.

"Goodnight Gorgeous."

"Goodnight."

If we began talking again for any reason, I would wait again for the silence and then say it once more and wait longingly for the reply.

"Goodnight Gorgeous."

"Goodnight."

Our date nights became even more special. When we first started, I really wanted this to be an important thing in our lives. I made a plan to take Laura out on a date every week. We were not rich, but this was going to be one of the things that I was willing to sacrifice for. We planned to go out every Monday night for four hours, from 6 to 10 PM. We had two children by this time and needed a babysitter, so I put the word out at our church and found a girl that agreed to watch them; not just once but every Monday night. I told her that if I cancelled on her, I would pay her anyway. It worked splendidly. I had to pay the babysitter, so there was very little chance that I was going to cancel my date night. I began to plan all my out-of-town business trips to start on Tuesday, never on Monday.

But every Monday night, after the date, after we were in bed and the time slowed down, when the quiet arrived, I would always end the night with those two words.

"Goodnight Gorgeous."

"Goodnight."

At first, the dates were dull and boring. We would go to the discount movie theater in hopes that it would take up time so we didn't have to sit and stare at each other for four whole long hours. We would go to dinner where we would split a hamburger and fries and two glasses of water...$10.00 with tip. I probably should have tipped more, but I did the math in my head and reasoned that I couldn't afford it. So we were careful not to ever ask for anything special or extra.

As time went on, our dates got better and better. We began talking and enjoying each other's company. We began hanging out at the mall, driving around the city and even taking walks all around our neighborhood. These weren't the "Honeymoon" kind of dates. We didn't walk around arm-in-arm feeling all gooey inside. No, these were just time together; not bad, but nothing I could really cheer about. I looked forward to them and I was sure Laura did too; but we were simply in a growing season, and we couldn't see the growth while we were in it.

I began realizing little things that I wanted to change about myself. I wanted to hold Laura's hand while we walked. We did for a while, but noticed that we had different strides in our walk and it wasn't comfortable for her. I was tall and she always had to hold her hand up instead of in its natural position, so that didn't quite work out. I began wearing the clothes that Laura thought looked good on me, some of which I really hated. I didn't think they looked good, but I reasoned that Laura was the only woman I wanted to impress...so I wore anything she suggested.

And then there was the ring....

Laura's wedding ring was a plain simple little thing that I was actually a little ashamed of. For a long time it was what we could afford; but it was never really what I wanted for her. I didn't need something huge to show off; I just wanted the ring to be a true symbol of my Love.

To me, the ring is a statement; not of price, but of identity. When my ring is placed on Laura, it tells everybody that she is mine; not like a possession but rather like a queen. It says that she has all rights and is acting with all of my authority in my kingdom. I had no idea what it meant to her, but that is what it meant to me. Later, I would find out how important it was to Laura to wear my ring and be under authority. It was a desire in her to have me declare that she is mine and that anything she says or does will be backed up by me. It was part of her security.

But Laura's ring wasn't anything like that. There was no power behind it because she knew that it had no value to me. I had another ring that I absolutely loved. It was beautiful with a large diamond on top; but it wasn't Laura's style. It was actually pretty gaudy so she wouldn't wear it. Besides, it would snag on her clothes and the gold prong that held the diamond on was constantly get caught on things and breaking off. She was afraid that the diamond would fall off and be lost, so that ring stayed locked up and she wore the other plain one.

I began asking her to wear the other ring on our dates. I would tell her it was just for the night and then she could change back to the other one. So she did. She didn't like it and worried about it, but she wore it on our dates...sometimes.

I took the ring to a jeweler and he changed out all the prongs for platinum that looked like gold. It cost me a little, but it took care of her worrying. He was also able to smooth out all the edges of the prongs and it stopped snagging on her clothing.

One year on our anniversary, I took her ring and had a smaller diamond added next to the large solitary one. I know...even more gaudy, but I thought it looked good.

A few years later, I did it again with a third diamond. She kept wearing it on dates and every once in a while to church, and soon it became her primary ring. Eventually, she got to the point that it was the only ring she would wear...the only ring she wanted to wear, and she was so proud to show it off. It wasn't the value of the ring; it really isn't that valuable compared to some others I have seen. It was the fact that it was mine, and I asked her to wear my ring. She had become mine.

The ring was beautiful, but she was Gorgeous. And every night, as the air got still and the world got quiet...

"Goodnight Gorgeous."

"Goodnight."

Brad's Shorts

Coffee in Weird Places

Years back, Laura and I began going to see movies on our date nights. It was great for us because we could just shut off the thinking part of our day and enjoy a respite of entertainment. We had our system: two tickets, large popcorn and large coke to share. We had our seats almost always in the same place, right in front of the rails separating the middle section from the walkway. This way, I could put my long legs up on the bars and nobody would get upset.

One night, as we were enjoying our popcorn we realized that the theater was cold. The air conditioner was on and blowing right on us. After suffering for 6-7 hours, I finally got up and went out to ask them to shut it off. They, of course, said that they would...but they didn't.

I was freezing. I had to do something. Going out to the lobby again, I looked around for an idea: a space heater, a blanket, matches, even two sticks to rub together...anything. Then I saw it. The letters that were perfectly shaped and distinguishingly black against a white background...COFFEE.

I thought to myself, "What a weird place for coffee."

I had never really thought about having coffee at a movie theater, but right now it sounded great. I forced my way to the front of the line, pushing an older lady in a wheelchair out of the way and hitting one guy in the back, knocking his soda out of his hands and to the floor. It was okay, he was not going to need a cold drink anyway. Once he got into the theater, he would realize this and probably thank me. I placed my order for one large cup of the heavenly nectar.

"That'll be $4.50, sir," said the girl just tall enough to see the numbers on the cash register.

"No, I just want one cup of coffee," I stated.

"Yes sir, it's $4.50."

"...For coffee?" I questioned.

She proceeded to tell me that this coffee was made by a company that sports a green mermaid on their cup. I didn't care if the coffee itself was made by mermaids. Now I understood why the air conditioners were on so high.

I paid the girl and got my coffee. Heading into the theater to share with my icicle wife, I decided to *get a few sips first. Standing right outside the door to our theater, I put the cup to my mouth and...burned my tongue. I spit coffee all over a picture of Marilyn Monroe.*

Speaking with a lisp, I mentioned too late to my wife that it was hot. We finished the movie with frozen feet and burnt mouths.

Upon leaving, I walked around the lobby and noticed that I could not find a sign anywhere that said,

"No Outside Food or Drinks."

I told Laura that we should bring our own coffee next time. She just laughed.

A few weeks later, another movie we wanted to see was showing at our theater so we made a plan to go. Laura came into the kitchen after getting ready for our date and found me brewing up the perfect pot of coffee.

"What are you doing?" she asked.

"I'm taking coffee to the movie. I realized that it is actually a great idea."

"Uhh, no, you're not," she said.

"Uhh, yes, I really am," I stated.

I poured the coffee into two thermoses and positioned them perfectly into the inside pockets of my large trench coat.

"Perfect."

"Those don't seal well," Laura said, half-laughing.

I twisted the top on with all my strength and headed for the door. We got in the car and I put the coffees into the cup holders between Laura and me. As we arrived at the theater, I noticed that I had forgotten to wipe the outside of the thermoses and now had excess coffee in the cup holder.

"I'll clean it later," I said to Laura, who rolled her eyes laughing at all that I was doing.

I placed the coffees into the inner pockets of my coat again, buttoned it up, fastened the belt around me and walked carefully upright to the ticket booth. I purchased our two tickets as Laura went in to buy our popcorn. The ticket guy handed me the tickets and the receipt just as a gust of wind caught one of the tickets and threw it to the ground.

I couldn't bend over. I'm not even sure I could squat down. I watched the ticket catch the breeze again and move about three feet away. I had no idea what I was going to do, when a young kid in line behind me chased it down and brought it back.

"Sir, you dropped this."

I acted as if I hadn't noticed and was so appreciative. He just looked at me with a really strange look on his face and ran back to his mom.

I headed for the door and realized that these coffees are making me warm inside this big overcoat. Just thinking about how hot the coffee was made me anxious to sit down and enjoy the spoils of this epic battle.

I headed up the ramp to the ticket collector and saw Laura already up there waiting. As I approached, I saw her eyes get bigger. She had just filled her mouth with popcorn and could only mumble. I was

pretty sure she was trying to tell me how much she loved me or how excited she was to see me, so I walked faster but still perfectly upright and not too jarringly. As I reached out to hand my tickets to the collector, I saw his eyes get big as well. He was staring at the waist of my overcoat. The thermoses were large against my stomach, so as I looked down to see what the issue was, I saw nothing. I was getting very hot in this coat but I looked normal.

He took my tickets and I passed by him with Laura following behind.

"Don't you feel that?" she asked.

"Feel what?" I said.

"I think your coffee leaked."

"Yeah, maybe a little. It's hard trying not to spill."

"Are you feeling a little hot?" she asked.

"Yeah, but this is my heavy coat. I'm going to take it off in the theater."

"I bet you are," she said.

We got to our usual seats and I opened my coat.

The thermoses had sealed perfectly. They did not leak a single drop out of the top. Unfortunately, they were both cracked on the bottom. Coffee had run out and down the entire front of my trench coat showing the world that I do not have control of my bladder. And because I was smart enough to cinch up my belt just below the thermoses, the coffee also ran perfectly into the top of my pants and down my legs.

"What a weird place for coffee," Laura laughed.

Chapter Eleven
And Then One Night

My wife loves plants. She loves to pot and re-pot them. She loves the idea of growth: flowers coming from the soil, leaves that are different from other leaves, and all kinds of biology and botany stuff. She was given a flowering plant a few years back from a friend. It sat on our kitchen counter for a few days and then was set out on the patio. It is a beautiful flower for about ten days a year, and then it goes back to just being a green stalky thing. In the winter it looks like a brown stick or is gone altogether. It always comes back and flowers the next year...if she takes care of it, feeds it, waters it, pulls it into the garage in the winter, keeps it in the shade and puts it out in just the right amount of sun. If the stars align and the moon is in just the right orbit, we get a flower for another ten days.

Seems like a lot of work to me, but she loves it.

It reminds me of when I was a child at my grandpa's house. My grandfather was a really neat man who loved to sit around and tell stories while he played cards, worked crossword puzzles and best of all, played dominoes.

I loved dominoes. Actually, I loved playing with dominoes, not playing dominoes. I don't like playing games. Board games, card games, all the different options; I don't enjoy them at all. But I loved setting up dominoes in a train to watch them fall. I would spend hours setting them up on the floor of my grandpa's living room. I would set them up in order: double blank first, then blank/one, blank/two and so on. If you do it right you can waste an entire day or more setting up dominoes. My grandparents lived in a mobile home retirement community and when somebody ran through the house, it shook the floor...in the living room. Dominoes would fall and I would get really upset. This was part of the challenge for me. Build it and knock it down before anybody else knocks it down. If I knocked it down myself prematurely, I would blame it on my brother for running in the house...or moving around too much...or just being there. Sorry, Brett.

After completing the whole set of almost one hundred double-twelve ivory pieces, I would step back and admire my handiwork. Then, I would knock it down by tapping the one piece on the end and watch them fall. In less than ten seconds it would all be over.

It didn't take me long to realize the there was a lot of effort being put into building this system for very little satisfaction. The enjoyment was good for a moment, but I remembered the work it took to get it and it wasn't worth the effort.

This is how I felt so often over the last fifteen years. My marriage was satisfactory, but I'm not sure that is the rating that a marriage should ever have. I didn't want to go through my life with a "satisfactory" marriage. The truth is...I hated the word. Even in school when I was very young we were given either an "S" for satisfactory or an "F" for failing on our report card. I would get in big trouble for getting an "F", but if I got a perfect card of all satisfactory, my dad would check it and say, "Okay."

No punishment, but no rewards. It was like a game that you couldn't win; just lose, or at best tie. I learned to hate the fact that I couldn't win. I hated "Satisfactory."

But somewhere over the years, I began to "reach the sink." Without even realizing it, my life with Laura had grown and become much better. We were talking more and ignoring each other less. We were fighting less and dating more, and we were actually enjoying it. The only problem was that I had this preconceived idea that I had I milk-toast marriage. Things had changed but because I was in the midst of them, I couldn't see it; so life just kept going on.

"Goodnight Gorgeous."

"Goodnight."

And then one night, we were climbing into bed and for some reason I noticed that Laura wasn't sleeping facing away from me. It hadn't been a particularly great day. I wasn't exceptionally nice to her today. We weren't fighting but we weren't necessarily honeymooners either. However, she was about to go to sleep lying on her back instead of facing the wall. I reached over to shut off the lamp next to our bed and I distinctly heard God speak to me again.

Softly, but in a very firm voice, these words broke through the darkness and caught me completely off guard.

> *"Tell her,*
> *Goodnight Gorgeous."*

"Uh, yeah...I know.
But I have to wait until
she's almost asleep."

I went on explaining to God that in order for it to work as planned, I have to wait until all the discussion is done and her breathing is almost rhythmic. That is when it has the most effect. I explained to God that I have been doing this for years. As a matter of fact, it has been eleven years. Wow! Has it really been that long?

Then God whispered again.

> *"Tell her,*
> *Goodnight Gorgeous."*

I sat there for a second and wondered if it was just my imagination; and maybe in my mind I was hearing

God say what I wished He would say. I reasoned with myself that I need to trust God no matter how odd it may be. I told myself that I would rather trust God and be wrong than be afraid to trust Him. So I did.

Lying there on my back, facing the ceiling with Laura just inches away from me, I spoke those same words out loud in my best "I Love You" tone.

"Goodnight Gorgeous."

"Goodnight," came the reply.

That was it, nothing special. We laid there in silence for a moment and I began deciding that I had not really heard God tonight. It had been so long since He told me anything new in this plan that I must have made it all up.

But then something happened.

In the motionless night, with nothing but the moonlight shining in through the blinds, I heard Laura speak the words that I didn't even know I was waiting for.

"You know," she said, "I can't even remember a time when you didn't tell me 'Goodnight Gorgeous'."

All of a sudden, I was flooded with all the memories of how different my marriage is now than it was when I started down this road. Somewhere on this journey, I finally reached the sink; I finally fit into those shoes; I finally fell in Love with my wife. And even more importantly, she fell in Love with me. We were friends again, not just friends, but Best Friends. She has become the person I want to be with more than anyone else. I love talking to her. I love just sitting and enjoying a cup of coffee with her. I love just being with her. I couldn't believe it. I was flooded with this deep feeling of Love for my wife, my bride, my Gorgeous Hottie.

I was so overwhelmed thinking about how God had done it, that I just laid there in silence and allowed the tears to fill my eyes. I'm not sure what else was said that night, if anything. I was so distracted with the fact that for the first time in my adult life and for the first time in my married life, I was happily married. It took me eleven years to get back the heart of the only woman I have ever Loved. God was so right. It was so simple, not easy. I knew that we were going to have a great marriage from now on, but this time I really knew it.

I spent the next few days walking around like an idiot with a huge grin on my face. I didn't care; life was so great. As I was driving in East Texas for work one afternoon, I was just talking out loud to God. He wasn't answering, but I knew He was listening. I was telling Him how thankful I was for all of my blessings and the thought crossed my mind to call my wife. I pulled the car over and we talked for about ten minutes. I told her how much I Loved her and assured her that I would be home late tonight. I hung up the phone and as I entered back onto the highway, I began hearing God again.

*"Now you are ready
to learn how to Love."*

My heart kind of sank a bit. I thought I was in a safe place. I thought Laura and I were going to be okay. I thought I had been learning and had learned. I took a deep breath and asked Him,

"Haven't I already learned how to Love Laura. I know I can always learn more, but...."

*"Son, you have been learning
how to Love her your way.
Now I'm going to teach you
how to Love her My Way."*

I had no idea at the time, but I was in the middle of the last conversation I would have with God for almost three years. I was completely enjoying where He had brought me so far and was actually excited about this new journey. I can handle anything. This might even be fun.

As I was driving down the highway, I yelled out loud,

"I'm ready!"

*"You know
I love you, right?"*

"Yes, I do."

*"You know I will never
leave you, right?"*

"Yes, I know."

*"You can talk with Me
anytime you want and
I will always hear you."*

"Okay...."

*"But anytime you want
to hear from Me,
go talk to Laura, because
I'm with her."*

The Gallbladder
I had the appendix removed.

Yelling From the Cheap Seats

When I was nine years old, my dad took me to see
the Heavyweight Boxing debut of Ed "Too Tall"
Jones. He was fighting a man named Abraham Yaqui
Meneses and it was going to be so great. This would be
my first foray into the world of the Boxing Spectator.
We gave the short, older guy at the entrance our tickets
and stopped by the refreshment stand for a coke and
some popcorn. And then...we entered into the main
area of the Pan American Center in Las Cruces, New
Mexico. It was huge. I was so excited to see all the
people, the lights and down in the middle...the boxing
ring. As I started heading down the steps to my
ringside seat that I thought had been reserved for me,
my dad called me back up to him and said we were

sitting over here, pointing up to a few seats behind him.

We climbed the cement steps for what might have been hours 'till we reached our destination: two seats right on the end of the row in the section closest to the ceiling.

There was no big screen TV to show me the action as it was happening. No...I had to squint and try to see what was going on. I knew it would be obvious to distinguish between the two fighters; Ed Jones would be the tall one, but I was so far away, I couldn't tell. As the fighting progressed, I had no idea what was going on. The crowd would cheer, and I would ask my dad what had happened. He would tell me some technical boxing lingo, but I'm pretty sure he had no idea either. He was sitting right next to me and there was no way he could tell what was going on.

I sat and watched my dad yell down, "Hit him!" and "Jab! Jab!" and "Keep your hands up!" along with all kinds of other phrases. Not knowing the exact situation or the plan that each fighter had already set out to complete, my dad was just shouting good ideas. It may not have been exactly applicable to either fighter, but it was still great advice. My dad wasn't part of their training, or even in a position of authority; he was just yelling from the cheap seats.

That is the position I am in right now. Laura and I currently work with troubled married couples and try and help them gain a foothold in their relationship. In the lives of these couples, we get to acquire lots of information about their marriages and their personalities.

I want so much to be able to help you but I have no idea what your situation is: whether you are married, divorced, remarried, widowed or single. I am, however, praying for you. I can't sit and visit with you and I can't glean any information about you or your marriage, but I can tell you some simple principles that God has led me in.

When I send text messages to my son, I will often have the caps locks on; it just looks cool. He usually reminds me that it means that I am yelling. So, I'm writing in all caps because with you, I feel like I'm YELLING from the cheap seats.

I hope you can hear me.

YOU ARE GOD'S FAVORITE CHILD

YOU DON'T NEED TO UNDERSTAND IT; YOU JUST NEED TO BELIEVE THAT GOD LOVES YOU MORE THAN ANYTHING. YOU ARE HIS BEST CREATION AND HE SMILES EVERY TIME HE THINKS ABOUT YOU. IF YOU HAD BEEN THE ONLY PERSON ON EARTH, CHRIST WOULD HAVE COME TO DIE JUST FOR YOU. HE LOVES YOU THAT MUCH. EVERYTHING GOD DID, DOES AND WILL EVER DO IS ALL WITH YOU IN MIND. YOU ARE HIS FAVORITE CHILD.

GOD WANTS TO BLESS YOU AND YOUR MARRIAGE

YOUR MARRIAGE IS A PICTURE OF YOUR RELATIONSHIP WITH GOD. HE WANTS TO SHOW YOU HOW MUCH HE CARES FOR YOU. NO MATTER HOW YOU FEEL ABOUT HIM, HE LOVES YOU ANYWAY. WHEN YOU'RE HAVING A BAD DAY, OR NOT IN THE MOOD TO TALK TO HIM, OR EVEN WHEN YOU ARE MAD AT HIM; HE NEVER QUITS LOVING YOU. HE WOULD CROSS THE OCEAN, MOVE A MOUNTAIN AND EVEN HANG THE MOON TO BLESS YOU, AND HE DID. HE IS THE PERFECT ONE TO LOVE YOU AND WANTS TO SHOW YOU THAT YOU ARE THE PERFECT PERSON TO LOVE THE SPOUSE THAT HE GAVE YOU.

ASK

THE FIRST PROBLEM THAT WE USUALLY SKIP OVER IS HOW TO GET HELP. THE BIBLE IS CLEAR,

> **"You do not have because you do not ask."(James 4:2)**

DON'T BE AFRAID TO ASK FOR HELP. ANYTIME I SEE SOMEBODY WHO OPERATES WELL IN AN AREA OF LIFE, BUSINESS OR

RELATIONSHIP IN WHICH I WOULD LIKE TO GET BETTER, I ASK THEM TO PRAY FOR ME. I BELIEVE THEY HAVE FOUND SOMETHING I WANT AND I ASK THEM TO GIVE IT TO ME. THEN I ASK THEM TO TEACH ME. GOD WANTS TO HELP YOU AND HAS SURROUNDED YOU WITH PEOPLE THAT WANT TO HELP YOU. HE DOES NOT EXPECT YOU TO CONQUER THIS YOURSELF; BUT YOU HAVE TO ASK FOR HELP.

BE STILL

FOR YEARS I TRIED SO MUCH AND WORKED SO HARD TO GET LAURA'S ATTENTION AND AFFECTION. I EVENTUALLY BECAME EXHAUSTED AND THAT IS WHEN GOD WAS ABLE TO BEGIN. SOMETIMES WE JUST NEED TO CALM DOWN, RELAX AND BE STILL. IF WE COULD BELIEVE THAT GOD IS ON OUR SIDE AND THAT HE IS AS GOOD AS HE SAYS THAT HE IS, THEN WE WOULD BE ABLE TO RELAX. WE WOULD BE AT PEACE KNOWING THAT THINGS ARE GOING TO WORK OUT JUST FINE. IF YOU LOVE GOD, THEN THE BIBLE IS TALKING ABOUT YOU WHEN IT SAYS,

...ALL THINGS WORK TOGETHER FOR GOOD TO THOSE WHO LOVE GOD... (Romans 8:28).

SOMETIMES WE JUST NEED TO BE STILL AND KNOW THAT HE IS GOD.

MEN WANT TO BE RESPECTED WOMEN WANT TO BE CHERISHED

AS I WAS WATCHING A TV SHOW ONE TIME, I HEARD A DAUGHTER ASK HER MOM WHEN SHE WOULD KNOW THAT THE TIME IS RIGHT TO HAVE SEX. THE MOM ANSWERED HER BY SAYING, "WHEN YOU LOVE HIM, BUT YOU HAVE TO MAKE SURE HE WILL STILL RESPECT YOU THE NEXT DAY." THAT IS EXACTLY OPPOSITE OF WHAT THE BIBLE SAYS. EPHESIANS TELLS US THAT MEN ARE TO LOVE THEIR WIVES AND WOMEN ARE TO RESPECT THEIR HUSBANDS. ISN'T IS JUST LIKE GOD TO CREATE A WOMAN AND THEN TELL A MAN EXACTLY WHAT SHE NEEDS IN ORDER TO FEEL LOVE...TO BE CHERISHED; AND TO CREATE A MAN AND TELL A WOMAN EXACTLY WHAT HE NEEDS TO FEEL LOVE...TO BE RESPECTED? GOD SAID,

LOVE NEVER FAILS (1Corinthians 13:8)

THEREFORE, ANY PERSON IN THE MARRIAGE CAN CHANGE THE DIRECTION AND THE OUTCOME OF THAT MARRIAGE JUST

BY LOVING THE OTHER PERSON THE WAY GOD INTENDED. WHEN SHE REPSECTS HIM, IT CAUSES HIM TO LOVE HER. WHEN HE CHERISHES HER, IT CAUSES HER TO REPSECT HIM. UNEXPLAINABLE, BUT IT WORKS.

SWEAT THE SMALL STUFF

AFTER LAURA AND I WERE FIRST MARRIED, I WAS READY TO MOVE ON TO OTHER THINGS. I DATED HER, IMPRESSED HER AND WON THE PRIZE. NOW, I CAN PUT MY MARRIAGE UP ON A SHELF AND GO CHASE OTHER DREAMS. IT WAS SO EASY TO STOP DOING ALL THE LITTLE THINGS I DID WHEN WE WERE DATING. I LATER REALIZED THAT THOSE "LITTLE THINGS" ARE WHAT CONTINUALLY SHOW HER MY LOVE. SHE LOVES IT WHEN I DO THE DISHES UNEXPECTEDLY. SHE HAS TO REDO THEM, BUT SHE APPRECIATES THE GESTURE. I LOVE IT WHEN SHE TURNS ALL THE LIGHTS ON IN MY OFFICE BECAUSE SHE DOESN'T WANT THE ROOM TO BE DEPRESSING FOR ME.

I KNOW WE HAVE BEEN TOLD NOT TO SWEAT THE SMALL STUFF IN LIFE, BUT IN YOUR MARRIAGE, THE SMALL STUFF IS HUGE.

NEVER, EVER, EVER GIVE UP

YOU HAVE A PROMISE FROM GOD THAT HE IS FOR YOU. HE IS ON YOUR SIDE. THE BIBLE TELLS ALL ABOUT HOW HE WANTS TO BLESS YOU AND PROSPER YOU. YOU HAVE TO DECIDE IF YOU BELIEVE THE WORD OF GOD. THE FACT IS: THE WORD OF GOD IS TRUE, NO MATTER WHAT YOU SEE, HEAR, FEEL, THINK OR SAY. THIS HAS BEEN ONE OF MY DAILY CONFESSIONS FOR YEARS NOW. EVEN WHEN YOU DON'T SEE THE RESULTS HAPPENING, OR YOU HEAR "FACTS" THAT DON'T ALIGN WITH IT, OR YOU DON'T FEEL ANY CHANGE, OR YOU THINK IT IS NOT WORKING OUT; AND EVEN WHEN YOU KEEP SAYING THAT IT CAN'T WORK, THE WORD OF GOD IS TRUE! HE SAYS YOU ARE MORE THAN A CONQUERER AND YOU ARE VICTORIOUS. NEVER QUIT. NEVER, EVER, EVER GIVE UP.

YA GOTTA YADA

THIS ONE IS IMPORTANT, MAYBE THE MOST IMPORTANT. YOU HAVE TO DO THIS. DON'T TRY TO MAKE IT WITHOUT THIS ONE. YA GOTTA YADA IS ALL ABOUT...

Read *I'm With Her* to find out!

From someone on the other side...
It is totally worth it!

Brad C. Engel

More to come in...

I'M WITH HER

FINDING GOD WHERE YOU NEVER EXPECTED

BRAD C. ENGEL

~ 137 ~

Tips from the Pros
Real People Who Have Overcome

"Put God first, marriage second and family third and take lots of vacations...together; and laugh at yourselves"

Neil and Dorothy Anderson
Motivational and Inspirational Coaches.
Married 40 years
Happily Married 40 years +/- one day

"Take turns hiding a small token of affection throughout the master bedroom. When your spouse finds it, they will know you were thinking of them."

Gorden & Kemberly McLaughlin
Real Estate Agents Dallas/Ft. Worth
Married 17 years
Happily Married 8 years

"Laugh! About everything. Don't take yourselves or life so seriously...and don't criticize! Just don't."
Gary and Lisa Moore
Logistics and Sales/Midland Texas
Married 20 years
Happily Married close to 20 years

"Have a regular date night where you concentrate on really talking to each other. Don't gripe about your spouse to your friends...and live in constant forgiveness."
Jim and Debbie Barber
Marriage Ministers Gateway Church
Married 35 years
Happily Married 20 years

"Serve each other (without) any competition. By definition, a fight is where somebody wins, somebody loses, and both get hurt. Don't go there."
Paul and Nancy Witt
Marriage Ministers Gateway Church
Married 45 Years
Happily Married most of the time

"Remember my heart; I would never do anything to hurt you. Run everything through this filter. Find things to do together that you both enjoy."

Garry & Ruth Barnes
Marriage Ministers Gateway Church
Married 22 years
Happily Married 8 years

"Never go to bed mad; try to make sure the kitchen sink is clean before bed so nobody wakes up to dirty dishes."

Duke Charles & Cory Engel
Author and Interior Designer/New Braunfels
Married 29 years
Happily Married a little less

"Speak words of life into each other, daily. Plan time together every day to talk, listen and especially dream."

Mike & Jeanne Preskenis
Marriage Ministers Gateway Church
Married 45 years
Happily Married 38 years

"Pray together, take walks, watch home movies, even do the dreary chores together and don't hold grudges."

Angel & Erika Rubalcava
Marriage Ministers Gateway Church
Married 30 years
Happily Married 20 years

"Always have something to look forward to as a couple. Set aside time for just the two of you to do things together. Don't try to fix or improve your spouse."

Bryan & Patti Tilbrook
Insurance and Wellness Consultant/Abilene
Married 32 years
Happily Married 30 years

I'm With Her

Coming soon to
Amazon, Barnes & Noble and
Everywhere great books are sold.

Find out more at:
BradCEngel.com

OTHER BOOKS BY BRAD ENGEL

Brad writes with his dad, Don Engel, under the pen name ***Duke Charles***. It has been a fantastic ride and they have thoroughly enjoyed working together. Don does almost all of the work and offered to let Brad take the credit for it...
big mistake.

LUKE KASH WESTERN SERIES
People of the Horse
Spirit and the Blood
Blood and Thunder
Thunder Cloud and Spirit Walker

ROC REESE MYSTERY SERIES
Birdies and San Diego Heat
Birdies and Vegas Heat
Birdies and Texas Heat
Birdies and New Orleans Heat

GIDEON, BOUNTY HUNTER

Are you married to a
Gorgeous Stud or a Gorgeous Hottie?
Declare it to the world with a

car sticker.
Free for a limited time at:
BradCEngel.com

For more information, other books by Brad C. Engel,
guest appearances, seminars or speaking engagements;
go to:

BradCEngel.com/contact.

Is pre-marital sex really that big a deal?
Go to:

BradCEngel.com/about

~ 147 ~

49704623R00094

Made in the USA
San Bernardino, CA
02 June 2017